NIGHT OF THE LONG KNIVES

Paul R. Maranin

THE NIGHT
OF THE
LONG
KNIVES

Forty-Eight Hours That Changed
the History of the World

PAUL R. MARACIN

THE LYONS PRESS
Guilford, Connecticut
An imprint of the Globe Pequot Press

To my wife, Kathryn, for her unflagging support
throughout this entire project.

The Lyons Press is an imprint of The Globe Pequot Press

10 9 8 7 6 5 4 3 2 1

Printed in the United States of America

Designed by Carol Sawyer of Rose Design

ISBN 1-59228-342-X

PHOTO CREDITS
Author photos: 121, 122, 137
Imperial War Museum: 13
David Gainsborough Roberts: 80
U.S. National Archives and Records Administration: vi, 2, 18, 22, 24,
26, 28, 32, 40, 52, 60, 64, 72, 78, 88, 94, 99, 100, 103, 106, 116, 124,
131, 132, 135, 138, 149, 152, 163, 167, 168, 176, 203, 205, 207

Library of Congress Cataloging-in-Publication Data is available on file.

What is evil lives forever.
—Spanish proverb

Acknowledgments

I am grateful for the assistance of my daughter, Paula Maracin-Krieg, whose assertiveness and German language fluency enabled me to personally retrace the steps of some of the perpetrators and victims of the Night of the Long Knives, especially at Bad Wiessee, Münich, Dachau, and Berchtesgaden. And I would be remiss not to recognize the contributions of my editor, Jonathan J. McCullough. His interest and suggestions were most helpful in preparing material for this book.

Contents

Robert Murphy. His early reports on Hitler to the State Department
received little interest. **viii**

Introduction

With the reunification of Germany, a tremor of trepidation rippled through Europe. International attention was again drawn to the legacy of Adolf Hitler, as the world well remembered what happened the last time Germany was united, its politics in a state of flux. How did it happen? Could it happen again? There was a period when many thought that it couldn't happen the first time.

The Nazi rule lasted twelve years and brought death and indescribable misery to countless millions. The worldwide conflict ignited by Hitler caused the death of approximately fifty million human beings. It is estimated that perhaps two-thirds of that incredible total were civilians. They were, in effect, all victims of one man. Some died in combat, some perished in death camps, others in bombed-out homes. Some drowned, some starved, while others froze to death. It would be virtually impossible to even guess the number of lives he deleteriously touched, in one way or another. Without Hitler running amok in Europe, would Japan have had the temerity to strike at Pearl Harbor in 1941?

Hitler was not exactly an overnight success story. It took years for him to reach the pinnacle, and along the way he made no secret of his goals. Robert Daniel Murphy became the consul general to Germany when the American consulate reopened in Münich in November 1921. He later wrote: "During my Münich years, I saw nothing to indicate that the American government or people were even mildly interested in the political developments which seemed so ominous and significant to us on the spot." According to Murphy, his messages did not stir any interest in the State Department, did not elicit any inquiries, and failed to evoke any response.

In the early 1920s an assistant military attaché at the American Embassy in Berlin, Army Captain Truman Smith, also had his eye on Hitler, whom he interviewed at length. In a written report, which was forwarded to Washington, Smith described the incipient Nazi Party as the "most active political force in Bavaria," and of Hitler, "the personality of this man has undoubtedly been one of the most important factors contributing to its success . . . His ability to influence a popular assembly is uncanny."

Murphy and Smith might as well have been reporting on obscure events in a remote Tibetan village for all the interest or concern educed from their superiors. Indeed, after the horrors of the First World War, America's foreign policy was dominated by a laissez-faire approach to Europe's problems, and Britain and France were on their own in rebuffing Germany's military resurgence. Regrettably, they were not up to the task. In the United Kingdom, Winston Churchill was one of the few voices raised in alarm as he recognized the peril posed by the Nazis. But he was still trying to recover from the stigma of Gallipoli, acquired while serving as First Lord of the Admiralty during World War I, and few paid attention to his warnings. Neville Chamberlain was the prime minister who dealt with Hitler. Chamberlain, with a background in business, was an advocate of orderly negotiation and diplomacy. Hitler, with a background in duplicity, believed in intimidation. It was a classic mismatch.

When Chamberlain returned from the infamous appeasement at München in 1938 with the German chancellor's signature on a piece of paper that was supposed to guarantee "peace in our time," he was cheered by Londoners who serenaded him outside of his residence at Number 10 Downing Street with "For he's a jolly good fellow." But the prescient Churchill lamented, "Britain and France had to choose between war and dishonor. They chose dishonor. They will have war." That meaningless "scrap of paper" is now on display in the Imperial War Museum in London, a reminder of man's gullibility. Many of the Londoners who raised their glasses to toast Chamberlain in 1938 were, in a few short years, desperately seeking shelter as the Luftwaffe soared overhead.

Hitler probably had an effect—directly or indirectly—on more people than any mortal who ever lived. He didn't do it alone, however. He had help from a cabal of pitiless men who formed his inner circle. It is not likely that fate will ever reassemble a similarly unique and sinister coterie.

They were essentially all losers, in the sense that all of them would have to be regarded as failures in the postwar German society that emerged from the ashes of the Great War. Not a one of them could satisfactorily earn a living as a civilian for a sustained period of time. They also shared another common ingredient: utter lack of compassion for their fellow human beings.

Yet these misfits were drawn together—with Hitler as the centerpiece—to form an ominous fraternity that would attract supporters like a magnet. Working tirelessly, they managed to wrest control of the National Socialist German Workers' Party and the government of Germany from opposing factions. Once they had the reins of control firmly in hand, it was as though they wanted to exact a vengeance upon society for the suffering and humiliation they had endured as nonentities during their own earlier days of deprivation and tribulation. While demanding sacrifice and hardship of the German populace, this arrogant clique exploited and abused the privilege of authority.

The primary purpose of this narrative is not to retell the story of Hitler's rise to power, although, perforce, the outline of that ascendancy is interwoven throughout the following pages. Rather, it is an attempt to place in perspective and historical juxtaposition an event that was to change the face of the earth and shape the course of history. It was the prelude to the Holocaust, and the precursor of what was to follow on a much larger and frightening scale. In many ways the civilized world is still paying the price.

Hitler became chancellor on January 30, 1933, but it wasn't until the early morning hours of June 30, 1934, that he set into motion an operation that in a mere forty-eight hours made him absolute master of Germany. It was a scenario that rivaled anything concocted on a Hollywood backlot: intrigue, betrayal, scheming, brutality, nefarious characters—and murder.

But it wasn't fiction. It really happened. And as a result, the stage was set for World War II.

The code name was KOLIBRI.

PART ONE

TRAVAIL AND ASCENT

In 1934 Franklin Delano Roosevelt was into the second year of a presidency that would span an unprecedented twelve years. There was talk about a "New Deal."

Americans were thoroughly enjoying Columbia Pictures' *It Happened One Night*, which won the Academy Award as the best motion picture of the year. The stars of the film, Claudette Colbert and Clark Gable, completed the sweep by garnering awards as best actress and actor of the year.

In a brief six-month period, law enforcement officers tracked down and shot to death five infamous outlaws who had attained almost folklorish status: Clyde Barrow and Bonnie Parker, John Dillinger, Pretty Boy Floyd, and Baby Face Nelson.

In Germany the new chancellor, Adolf Hitler, was beginning to flex his muscles. Europe had little inkling of what lay ahead.

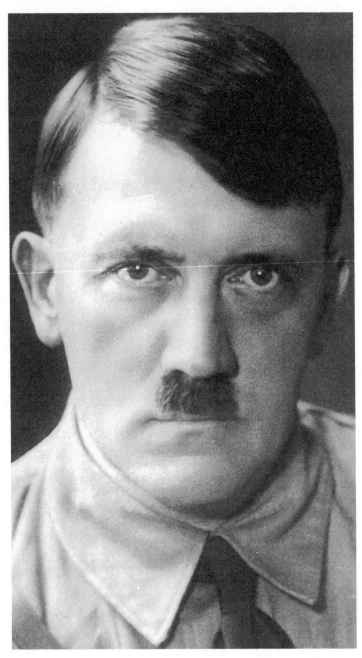

Adolf Hitler

Chapter 1

THE PROTAGONIST EMERGES

On June 30, 1934, American foreign correspondent William L. Shirer was in Paris. He made an entry in his diary on that date, which read in part as follows: "Berlin was cut off for several hours today, but late this afternoon telephone communication was reestablished. And what a story! Hitler and Göring have purged the SA, shooting many of its leaders . . . The French are pleased. They think this is the beginning of the end for the Nazis."

In retrospect, this could be classified as perhaps the most palpable miscalculation in the annals of recorded history. What the French could not have foreseen was that the shots being fired in Germany that day were, in effect, the opening salvos of a global war. In just six traumatic years, apprehensive Parisians would watch in disbelief as Nazi columns triumphantly marched down the tree-lined Avenue des Champs-Elysées and the Gestapo became ensconced at 72 Avenue Foch. Near Limoges, the inhabitants of Oradour-sur-Glane did not realize that their village was destined for eradication and would cease to exist in exactly ten years to the month. In Germany—behind a screen of secrecy—unfolding was a grim drama that would presage ultimate suffering and death for untold millions throughout the unwary world.

The year before, in January 1933, Adolf Hitler, age forty-three, had taken the oath of chancellor, culminating a long and devious climb to power. Who was this person who would bring ruin and opprobrium to the country that had produced Kant, Beethoven, and Göthe?

He wasn't even a German. He was born April 20, 1889, in the Austrian town of Brannau am Inn, the son of a minor customs official named Alois Hitler who in early life was known as Alois Schickelgruber. An indifferent student, he chafed under a domineering father who wanted him to become a civil servant. In later life he took every opportunity to castigate the schoolteachers who had tried to educate him, referring to his former instructors variously as "mentally deranged," "congenital idiots," or "absolute tyrants." It was obvious that he did not reflect upon his school days with much affection.

Hitler was thirteen years old when his father died in 1903, and from then on he became the responsibility of his hard-pressed mother, Klara, who had a tendency to coddle young Adolf. With a strong father figure removed from the scene, Klara experienced considerable difficulty in keeping her troubled son interested in school. Klara wanted him to fulfill his father's wish and become a member of the civil service, which would have provided a degree of stability and a steady income. Adolf thought further schooling would somehow interfere with his ambiguous goal of becoming an artist. His continued attendance at the government science high school in Linz was an unhappy experience. He flunked the French examination, necessitating a repeat test which he barely passed. The professor who administered the French examination, Dr. Eduard Hümer, would later say: "Hitler was definitely talented although he was rather one-sided, and he really didn't have that one side under control either. He was obstinate, high-handed, dogmatic, and irascible, and found it very difficult to fit into a school situation. He simply wasn't diligent." In plain words, he was a nonconformist. Some aspects of his adolescence would follow him through adult life.

To complete his high school education, his mother sent him off to the State Senior High School in Steyr. However, his formal schooling ended when he dropped out of that school before qualifying for graduation. During his time in Steyr, he found lodging with a court official named Conrad Edler von Cichini. (The house, located at 19 Grünmarkt, would later be designed a landmark by the Nazis, replete with appropriate plaque.)

Back in Linz, Hitler resumed residence under his mother's roof and enjoyed the life of an idler. His mother provided for his needs, and from her meager widow's pension even gave him enough money for a tailor-made wardrobe. He started carrying a walking stick and would often be seen eating sweets at the local Café Baumgarten, to the astonishment of his former classmates from the Linz schools.

In the fall of 1907 the eighteen-year-old aspiring artist journeyed to Vienna to take the entrance examination at the Academy of Fine Arts. He survived the initial six-hour phase (while thirty-three applicants did not), but failed to pass the second segment. This is not to say that he was completely without talent in this field. Many of the applicants were accepted or rejected solely on the whims of the various examiners. Interestingly, Robin Christian Andersen, who later became director for the School of Masters Painting at the Vienna Academy of Fine Arts, also failed to pass the same examination that Hitler took. The world can wonder how history might have been affected had Hitler been favored with a passing grade and accepted as a pupil.

Acquiescing to the chagrined Hitler's request, the Jewish president of the Academy, Professor Seigmund L'Allemand, met privately with Hitler. Far from discouraging the young hopeful, L'Allemand suggested that he submit an application to the Academy's School of Architecture, as his illustrations, in the opinion of the professor, reflected some aptitude in that particular area. Hitler found out the next day that his lack of a high school diploma precluded his enrollment in the architectural classes. The folly of his earlier decision to drop out of school had now come home to haunt him.

Thoroughly rebuffed, an embittered Hitler returned to Linz to find his mother dying of cancer. Her death on December 21, 1907, left him on his own. His indolent lifestyle, pursued at his mother's expense, had failed to prepare him for the real world. He didn't have a trade. He had nothing to offer an employer, even if he had wanted to look for a job—which he didn't. But he was not entirely without funds. He was the recipient of approximately 130 crowns a month, derived from his parents' inheritance and an "orphan allowance."

In January 1908 Hitler returned to Vienna. Compared to the provincial town of Linz, the Austrian capital was another world. Vienna was a pulsing, fascinating city in motion, and it was into this atmosphere that the ill-equipped

Hitler plunged. He rented a room at 29 Stumpergraße, which he shared with a friend named August Kubizek. He made another attempt to enroll in the Vienna Academy of Fine Arts, but this time (after showing samples of his work), he wasn't even permitted to take the examination. This was the final blow to his artistic aspirations, and on November 18, 1908, he changed his place of residence to Room Number 6 at 22 Felber Street. With his inheritance monies gradually diminishing, Hitler (who had registered with police authorities as a student) moved with increasing frequency, continually seeking cheaper accommodations. As was the custom in Vienna, every time he moved he was required to register his new address with the police. On August 20, 1909, he temporarily moved into a working-class district at 58 Sechshauser Street, about the time he received notice to report for military induction. When his monthly twenty-five-crown orphan allowance ended, probably because of his frequent residence changes, his situation became critical. His slide into social disrepute had begun. He eschewed regular employment or learning a trade, while drifting about Vienna, sitting on park benches, sleeping in doorways and flophouses, and frequenting night shelters where he was given soup and bread. He was not averse to begging in lieu of manual labor, which he assiduously avoided.

While staying at the Meidling homeless shelter near the southern railroad station, Hitler met another habitué of the streets named Reinhold Hanisch, who had experience as a graphic artist. The two became friends and earned modest amounts of money carrying luggage at various railroad stations. At Hanisch's urging, they formed somewhat of a partnership, with Hitler painting postcards and Hanisch selling them to customers in the many taverns and cafés that dotted Vienna. Their arrangement called for a fifty-fifty split of the receipts. In February 1910 the two neophyte entrepreneurs moved to the Men's Home on Meldemann Street in the Brigittenau Section, a city-owned boardinghouse for single men. Compared to Hitler's most recent residences, this facility was almost elegant.

Hitler and Hanisch gradually built up their business, and soon graduated to painting and selling larger pictures that would fit into frames. This way, they could sell the paintings to frame dealers who needed an inexpensive picture to fit into frames—a gimmick designed to enhance the probability of frame sales. Not unexpectedly, Hitler and Hanisch had a disagreement; Hanisch accused Hitler of laziness and unwillingness to cooperate, and Hitler claimed that Hanisch was cheating him out of his fair share of the profits. The dispute culminated in August 1910, when Hitler filed a complaint with the police station in Brigittenau, accusing his erstwhile partner of "embezzlement of fifty crowns in the form of a picture that was to be sold."

On the basis of this pleading, Hanisch was prosecuted, convicted, and sentenced to a week in jail. As Hanisch was placed in custody, he railed at Hitler, in effect, threatening to "even the score" if he ever had the opportunity. Fate would decree otherwise. It would take twenty-eight years, and Hanisch, instead of evening the score, would pay the penalty for crossing the failed artist.

Hitler continued his checkered lifestyle in Vienna, and in May 1913, he notified the police that he was moving to Münich, where he established his abode with a tailor named Popp at 34 Schleißheimer Street. Up until this point he had successfully dodged the Austrian draft. However, in June 1913 (at the request of the Austrian police), a Münich police officer arrested Hitler. After a night in jail, he appeared before the Austrian consul in Münich who ordered him to report for his induction examination in Salzburg. He was rejected for military service, with the explanation: "Unfit for general and limited service; too weak."

The change of scenery from Vienna to Münich did not modify his aversion to steady employment as he continued his indolent, bohemian lifestyle. Political discussion (or argument) was the only stimulant that aroused his interest. At this stage of his life he had experienced utter failure in everything he had attempted. Could anyone in their wildest nightmare have dreamed that this unkempt drifter would one day occupy the position held by Bismarck?

In Sarajevo, Bosnia, on June 28, 1914, the Archduke Franz Ferdinand, heir to the Hapsburg throne, was assassinated by a Serbian student named Gavrilo Princip, and war fever was beginning to permeate Austria and Germany. World War I was on the horizon, a catastrophe that would mark a turning point in Hitler's life and provide him with his first full-time job. There would be no more sleeping in parks and scrounging for food. For the first time since he had left the sanctuary of his mother's home, he would be assured of food, clothing, and shelter. As "the guns of August" prepared to boom, the twenty-five-year-old Austrian misfit volunteered for duty with the Bavarian Army.

The business of war seemed to appeal to him, and for the first time in his life he was doing something that provided gratification. He became a regimental staff runner with the First Company of the 16th Bavarian Reserve Infantry, known as the List Regiment, named after its first commander, Colonel von List. This regiment was made up mostly of intellectuals and students who had volunteered for active duty, and through questionable leadership the ranks sustained severe loss of life. While working as an orderly to Lieutenant-Colonel Freiherr von Tubeuf, Hitler had occasion to be in the regimental commander's office one day when a young officer named Rudolf Hess walked in. They looked at each other. It is unknown whether or not they spoke. Could Hess have envisaged the impact this insignificant orderly would have on his personal destiny in just a few short years?

During his war-time service Hitler was wounded twice, was gassed, and was awarded the Iron Cross, both First and Second Class. Although he acquired a reputation as a reliable runner, he did not advance beyond corporal. The consensus of his superiors was that he could not command respect if promoted to sergeant.

The collapse of the German military forces in late 1918 and the termination of armed conflict would return Hitler to a realm he feared—civilian status. The cessation of hostilities had thrown Germany into chaos and bitterness, and it was into this maelstrom that ex-serviceman Hitler now stepped. He had decided to become a politician.

Germany at this juncture was being buffeted by forces from both the extreme left and extreme right. Unemployment, frightful inflation, and anarchy reigned. Communist sympathizers were making their move. As a protest against four years of futile and enervating warfare, resentful civilians were attacking returning servicemen in uniform. The Freikorps (Free Corps), a volunteer quasi-military organization, was established by some of these former soldiers for self-protection and to resist the steadily increasing influence of the Communists. There was social, political, and economic upheaval. The climate was inviting to a clever demagogue, and against this volatile backdrop the political career of Hitler was launched.

The forerunner of the Nazi Party was a small, disorganized group called the German Workers' Party, founded by Anton Drexler, with the assistance of Karl Harrer (the latter, of all things, a sports writer). Their cash depository was a cigar box. Hitler attended his first meeting of this minuscule organization even before his reentry into civilian life. The turmoil that gripped Germany during this tumultuous period was almost unimaginable. Law and order virtually disappeared, and the Freikorps, in the role of vigilantes, killed people indiscriminately, as the official government, what was left of it, struggled to maintain a semblance of order. In Münich, bodies littered the street and unidentified victims were buried in mass graves to prevent the spread of disease. American newspaperman Ben Hecht (of *The Front Page* fame) was in Germany as a foreign correspondent for the *Chicago Daily News* from December 1918 through early 1920, and he had a front-row seat. He cabled his editor: "There is nothing sane to report." During this epochal time Hitler was an unknown. But he was there—and he was far from inactive. This was the incubation period that nurtured the genesis of World War II and the Holocaust.

In the army, a bureau was established to identify and investigate political activities of a subversive nature. Captain Karl Mayr was placed in charge of this section, and it was his duty to select the men who would staff this newly formed intelligence unit. One of his recruits was a young enlisted man awaiting discharge. His name was Adolf Hitler. As far as history is concerned, it was a calamitous selection.

It was in the autumn of 1919 that Hitler, pursuant to orders, joined a paltry twenty-three participants in a meeting of the German Workers' Party. He was supposed to be an observer, but he ended up an avid member. On the first day of 1920 he was issued a membership card. After his discharge from the service on March 31, 1920, he became totally engulfed in the fortunes and progress of the party. In Münich, he rented a sparsely furnished room from a Mrs. Reichert at 41 Thiersch Street in the Lehel section. It had been nine months since the Treaty of Versailles was officially signed, imposing rigorous and humiliating terms upon Germany. The Kaiser had fled to Holland. There was no Marshall Plan. The victorious Allies were in no mood to extend assistance to the thoroughly vanquished Germany and its disintegrating political and economic structure. The attitude toward the defeated Germans seemed to be that they deserved it.

Hitler now had party affiliation. The German Workers' Party and Hitler would never be the same again. Already a member of this fledgling party was Ernst Röhm, a captain on active duty with the Reichswehr (Regular Army). Röhm was to play a decisive role in the formation and direction of the Third Reich.

Hitler was now given opportunities to deliver speeches as a representative of a political party with an agenda, and he took full advantage of every chance that presented itself. His speeches during this stage of his political nonage usually consisted of attacks on two primary targets: the Treaty of Versailles and the Jews. This was too much for sportswriter Harrer, and he resigned his chairmanship of the party. Hitler's flair for oratory came into full play as he relentlessly expounded his views and prejudices, intermixed with bitter denunciations. The time would come, Hitler intoned, "when the banner of our movement will fly over the Reichstag, over the Castle in Berlin, yes, over every German house." Few believed him, but he was speaking the truth. One of his early biographers, Konrad Heiden, wrote: "Anyone acquainted with the unhappy life of this lonely man knows why hatred and persecution guided his first political footsteps. In his heart he nursed a grudge against the world, and he vented it on guilty and innocent alike."

As he solidified his position, Hitler also took over the party's propaganda activities, thus initiating the method of operation that would prove to be so successful for him. His technique was to usurp authority and attain a certain goal, and then deny that same avenue to others.

In April 1920 the name of the organization was changed to the Nazional Soziolistische Deutsche Arbeiter Partei (NSDAP), or the National Socialist German Workers' Party. This was the Nazi Party. There were two significant developments in 1921: Hitler became chairman of the expanding party, and the so-called "Brownshirts" came into existence. They were labeled the *Sturmabteilung* (Storm Detachment), or SA. This strong-arm unit of storm troopers was initially formed to protect party functions from "outside interference," and they did their job well.

Sturmabteilung recruiting poster: "Service with the SA raises one to comradeship, toughness, and strength." On June 30, 1934, it also meant death.

The new chairman was in his element before a crowd, but in small intimate groups he was an awkward, embarrassed social misfit, lacking confidence in one-on-one confrontations with knowledgeable conversationalists. This would change in later years after he had gained authoritarian control over others and did not have to brook any divergence of opinion.

Working zealously and tolerating no opposing views from within the party, Hitler could count on 55,000 supporters as the autumn of 1923 arrived. He now decided—improvidently—on an audacious move. He would seize control of the Bavarian state government by force. Thanks to the efforts of Röhm, the SA was now 15,000 strong and straining at the leash. What followed on November 9, 1923, was the ill-fated, oft-cited, and farcical "Beer Hall Putsch." During this premature adventure, a cordon of outnumbered state policemen armed with carbines fired on the advancing line of revolutionaries led by Hitler, Hermann Göring, and General Erich Ludendorff (an early supporter of Hitler) as the rebels marched defiantly down a Münich street. As they approached the Odeonsplatz, shots rang out, and Hitler hit the ground as his columns disintegrated wildly, scattering in all directions to avoid the police bullets. Hitler was the first to break ranks and run for cover, making his escape in a yellow Opel parked nearby with the motor running. Sixteen Nazis and three policemen died in the brief encounter. Hitler's rash attempt to stage a revolution had been summarily crushed, and two days later the fugitive party leader was located and placed under arrest. He soon found himself in the dock as one of ten defendants charged with high treason (Göring and Hess had fled to Austria).

The trial—which was a travesty—began on February 26, 1924, and was held in People's Court I located in a former infantry school on Blutenburg Street in Münich. It was given considerable coverage by the media, which provided the opportunistic Hitler with still another platform. The defendants appeared before a panel of five judges, three of whom were laymen. The presiding magistrate was Justice George Neithardt, who permitted Hitler to interrupt proceedings at will. The panel demonstrated partiality by favoring defense witnesses. One observer saw the trial as "a farce that made Bavaria the laughing stock of the world." A key prosecution witness was Gustav von Kahr, the Bavarian State Commissioner General. His testimony would cost him his life. Hitler was permitted to turn the proceeding into a political sideshow. His opening statement, for instance, lasted four hours, and he was given wide latitude in cross-examination. The prosecutor (obviously sympathetic to Hitler) did not enhance the strength of his case by frequently praising Hitler during the twenty-four-day trial. Nevertheless, the Nazi Party chief was found guilty and a minimum five-year sentence imposed with the understanding he would be eligible for early parole consideration.

Hitler emerged from the trial as a political martyr, and he was transferred to Landsberg Prison to serve his term of confinement under less than onerous conditions. During his imprisonment—ensconced in comfortable quarters—he started working on his book *Mein Kampf* (My Struggle), with the help of Rudolf Hess who had returned from Austria. The book's central theme seemed to be the victory of the strong over the weak, with concomitant disdain for individual rights. He made it clear that he was not interested in any form of democracy or any manner of government in which the oppressed would have redress.

While Hitler was out of circulation, his party began to splinter into several competing factions. It virtually fell apart without the dictatorial stewardship of the prisoner of Landsberg, who reposed in his cell, contemplating his future.

Chapter 2

INTO THE DRIVER'S SEAT

When he was released from prison on December 20, 1924, Hitler found a Germany that was—with the influx of foreign investments—slowly recovering its economic stability. The catastrophic inflation had been curbed and unemployment reduced. This was good for Germany but bad for Hitler because it was not the type of political environment in which his demagoguery could flourish. To compound his difficulties, the Nazi Party had been banned. To many of his critics it seemed that the Hitler era had come to an end, and that he would be deemed just another rabble-rouser relegated to political oblivion. But he had other ideas. The unsuccessful revolt had forced him into another decision. He would abandon the "violent

Gregor Strasser. His allegiance to Hitler cost him his life.

overthrow" approach to power. He would now work within the system, and he proceeded to do just that. In the end, he would destroy the system and all who dared oppose him.

Gregor Strasser, a graduate of the University of Münich where he had majored in chemistry and pharmacy, had originally joined the Nazi Party in 1920, and he was now moving into a position of strength in party matters. With the party in disarray during Hitler's incarceration at Landsberg, Strasser had sought and won a seat in the Reichstag in the spring of 1924 under the aegis of the National Socialist German Freedom Movement. But in March 1925 he returned to the Nazi Party, at Hitler's beckoning. The burly ex-Army lieutenant, who had also won the Iron Cross, First Class, became a threat to Hitler's leadership and began to attract a sizable following. He did not agree with Hitler on many issues, and more often than not advanced his own independent views which were decidedly socialistic. Assisted by Otto, his younger brother, Strasser commenced to build a political base in Northern Germany. He founded the newspaper *Berliner Arbeiterzeitung*, (Berlin Workers' Paper), and Otto became editor.

In addition to fundamental ideology, the Strasser brothers differed with Hitler on another important point. Their motive was to use the party to further socialist aims and to achieve what they considered necessary governmental reforms, albeit radical. Hitler's motive was to utilize the functions of the party as instruments with which to further his personal ambition of becoming a dictator. He did not want to reform government. He wanted to demolish it and supplant it with his own brand of totalitarianism. These two views were, of course, incompatible as well as irreconcilable, as the Strassers would tragically realize at a later date.

In Bavaria, Hitler began the painstaking reconstruction of his domain. He managed to have the ban on the party rescinded as of January 1, 1925, but he himself was prohibited from public speaking for a two-year period because of the inflammatory nature of his oratory. He continued to speak before party gatherings, however, and inevitably undermined the Strasser wing to the extent that he lured most of Strasser's supporters (as well as Gregor himself) into his fold. He would even become godfather to Gregor's twin sons, Günther and Helmuth. Such was the almost hypnotic persuasion Hitler could exert. Otto would never be converted, although he had to concede that Hitler's fiery dramatics before a crowd would stir him despite his realization that most of what he heard was meaningless rhetoric.

By early 1926 Hitler had regained complete control over the party, and by year's end the official membership stood at approximately 50,000 supporters. The SA was becoming increasingly important as Hitler's private enforcement arm. During the late 1920s the rule seemed to be that when Germany's fortunes rose, Hitler's sank. His type of appeal feasted on adversity. The more discouraged the working class became, the more support Hitler attracted. To enable his program to work within the system, he created an elaborate party structure, encouraging citizenry from all sectors of society to become associated with the Nazis, including women and teenagers. His aim, of course, was to garner votes—votes to put his representatives in the Reichstag. He was ineligible to run for office himself because he was not a German citizen. It was not until 1932 that he became a naturalized citizen.

By 1928 the Nazi Party boasted 108,000 dues-paying members, and in the Reichstag elections in May of that year the party received 810,000 votes, which translated to twelve seats in the 491-member Reichstag. It was the foot in the door Hitler had been seeking.

By 1930, Hitler would neutralize the Strasser wing of the party. Otto, through his newspaper, continued to espouse the principles of socialism and the nationalization of industry, while Hitler tried to mollify the uneasy industrialists who threatened to discontinue financial support unless Otto was silenced. After a stormy confrontation with Hitler at the Sans Souci Hotel in Berlin, Otto Strasser was expelled from the party on July 4, 1930. In a poignant parting, Gregor firmly gripped his brother's hand and told him that his political allegiance would remain with Hitler. Ultimately, Otto would flee and live; Gregor would stay and die.

In October 1929 the crash on Wall Street shook the international financial establishment, and the ripple effect soon reached Europe—especially Germany. In 1930 the German economy faltered as the worldwide depression began to immerse the developed countries. Inversely, the coffers of the Nazi Party (no longer a cigar box) swelled as largesse in the form of financial contributions from wealthy industrialists materialized. The loss of foreign investors (mostly American) and the curtailment in world trade helped propel Germany into a tailspin, although the full impact of the depression did not hit Germany until 1931.

In 1932 Hitler made his first and only run for an elective office as he decided to challenge a legend at the polls. On February 22 he announced his candidacy for the presidency of Germany, opposing the aging incumbent, Field Marshal Paul von Hindenburg. Von Hindenburg had become a German national hero as a result of his military service during World War I. Although vastly outnumbered, he was credited with masterminding the victory

Hans Baur

over a Russian force at the Battle of Tannenberg in August 1914. In August 1916 he became supreme Commander of all German armies. He subsequently emerged from retirement and was elevated to the presidency in May 1925.

A massive, whirlwind campaign was launched, and Hitler took to the air. It was at this time that Hans Baur entered the picture. Baur had been a fighter pilot in World War I, and had ended up a squadron leader. After the war he became a military airmail pilot, and when Lufthansa was established as a German airline in January 1926, he was among their very first pilots, advancing to flight captain in 1928. In March 1932 he was screened by Hitler in a meeting at Nazi headquarters in the Brown House in München. Hitler had decided to rent an airplane for campaigning throughout Germany, and sought an experienced and dependable pilot he could trust. An acquaintance had recommended Bauer, and as a result of this session Baur became Hitler's personal pilot and would remain so until the bitter end.

Hitler was probably the first major politician to use aircraft as a means of reaching voters, and on his initial flight across Germany he visited twenty-one towns in seven days. His frenzied speech making would often leave him limp and soaked with perspiration. The loyal Gregor Strasser threw himself into the intensive campaign by delivering a series of speeches on Hitler's behalf, while his brother Otto urged Hitler's defeat. Otto incurred the Nazi leader's everlasting enmity when, in a speech at Stuttgart, he quoted Hitler's confidential remarks to him that Germany needed a government *over* the people and not a government *of* the people.

During this presidential campaign an interesting sidelight developed that revealed Hitler's inferiority complex when it came to personally dealing with anyone he

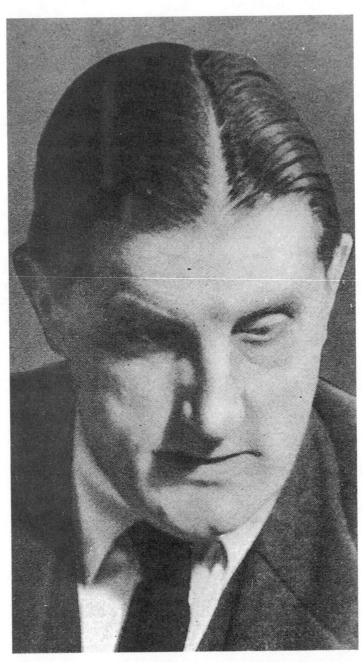

Dr. Ernst "Putzi" Hanfstängl. He failed to lure Hitler to Winston Churchill's dinner table at Münich's Hotel Continental.

considered his equal or better. He was comfortable before a large audience of strictly listeners, or in a small group of sycophants, but it was another story when it came to dialogue with strong personalities whose views might differ from his own. It so happened that in the month of April 1932 Winston Churchill and his wife visited Münich for a few days, and the former First Lord of the Admiralty expressed an interest in meeting the ambitious office seeker who had the temerity to run against the Hero of Tannenberg.

Churchill's son, Randolph, attempted to set up the meeting by contacting Ernst "Putzi" Hanfstängl, the Harvard-educated aide who was Hitler's buffer with foreign journalists. Hitler and Hanfstängl were invited to join the Churchill family for dinner at the Hotel Continental. Hanfstängl tried to convince Hitler that he should not miss the opportunity to exchange ideas with one of England's most knowledgeable and influential politicians, but Hitler would have no part of it. He at first offered the lame excuse that he would have nothing to talk to him about, and then said he was too busy, but it was obvious to Hanfstängl that Hitler was afraid to be alone with Churchill, and to be tested under these one-on-one circumstances.

As it was, Hanfstängl joined the Churchills for dinner at the appointed hour without Hitler. Interestingly, Hitler was at the hotel later that evening on other business and Hanfstängl chanced to encounter him in the hallway. Hitler rebuffed Hanfstängl's further efforts to lure him to Churchill's nearby table, and—on the pretext that he was unshaven—backed away and hurriedly exited the hotel. Thus, by the thinnest of margins, historians were denied the intriguing vignette of an informal peacetime meeting of two of the world's foremost adversaries.

Winston Churchill succeeded the ailing Neville Chamberlain as
Prime Minister on May 10, 1940.

After a run-off election in April, the results were tabulated. Despite the fact that he was receding into senility, the feeble von Hindenburg had handily beaten his rival by almost six million votes. It was a bitter defeat for Hitler that sent him back to the drawing board.

Germany was gradually reverting to a chaos reminiscent of the dark days that followed the end of World War I. There was a renewal of violence in the streets as the SA—now 400,000 strong—under Ernst Röhm created havoc. The Reichstag was dissolved a number of times, and within a period of five months there were three national elections. A succession of ineffective chancellors appointed by President von Hindenburg added to the confused political atmosphere as intrigue followed upon intrigue. In a nation without a tradition of democracy, the idea of responsible officeholders representing the interests of a constituency was a concept of government the politicians and the electorate did not seem to comprehend.

In the elections of November 6, 1932, the Nazi Party won 196 seats (out of 584) in the Reichstag. Although it was a net loss of seats from the previous election, the Nazis were still the largest party in that chamber, but still considerably short of a majority. The president had at one time firmly stated that he would offer Hitler a post no higher than the post office ministry, but now amidst the shifting sands of politics and pressure exerted by his advisers, he relented and offered him the chancellorship—if he could produce a workable parliamentary majority in the Reichstag. This Hitler could not do, and he refused to consider a coalition that would lessen his control. Hitler sensed that his hour was approaching.

Maneuvering continued, and on December 2, von Hindenburg appointed Lieutenant General Kurt von Schleicher as chancellor, replacing the inept Franz von Papen

Joachim von Ribbentrop (right) with Adolf Hitler

(the president's next-door neighbor in Berlin). Von Schleicher, who had an in with the president as a result of friendship with von Hindenburg's son, had been a canny, behind-the-scenes manipulator for some time and had kept the political pot boiling by advising the president on key appointments. Von Schleicher's tenure as chancellor would be short-lived.

In an effort to isolate Hitler, von Schleicher in a bold move offered Gregor Strasser the vice-chancellorship in his cabinet. This was an affront to Hitler, as normally this offer would have been extended to the party head. Hitler was infuriated at this unexpected development, and in an acrimonious meeting with Strasser on December 7, 1932, not unlike a similar confrontation with his brother Otto two years earlier, Hitler accused the startled Gregor of disloyalty, treachery, and conspiracy. After devoting ten years of his life to the cause of the party, the disillusioned Strasser relinquished his seat in the Reichstag and resigned from all offices in the Nazi Party. Belatedly, he realized he had been in league with the devil.

Von Schleicher, for all of his deviousness and artful persuasion, could not inveigle the backing he needed in the Reichstag to effectively govern or survive, to the disappointment of von Hindenburg. Von Papen was unrealistically entertaining hopes of regaining his lost chancellorship. Gregor Strasser had removed himself from contention just as his party was at the threshold. Hitler emerged as the compromise candidate for the job.

With the finish line in sight, Hitler pulled out all the stops. After winning over von Papen, he then adroitly played his trump card. He arranged—through von Papen—to meet with Colonel Oskar von Hindenburg, the son and adjutant of the rapidly fading eighty-six-year-old president. The clandestine session was held on the wintry night of January 22 at the plush home of Joachim von Ribbentrop, a wine and spirits importer who would later become Hitler's undiplomatic foreign minister. No one knows what was said or promised at this private meeting, but before the evening was over Hitler had the crucial support of the younger von Hindenburg. The unthinkable was about to happen.

Eight days later—January 30, 1933—Hitler was named Chancellor of the Reich.

Berlin was in a festive mood, with mass demonstrations and torchlight parades staged by the triumphant Nazis and their ecstatic followers. According to his book *Flight from Terror*, Otto Strasser stood unnoticed on a street corner on the Wilhelmstraße and shivered in the brisk night air as he watched the celebrants.

They were dancing at their own funeral.

Chapter 3

THE SOLDIER

As the year 1934 began, Ernst Röhm was riding the crest of success in Berlin. He was chief of staff of the SA, and, more than any other single individual, he was responsible for Hitler's rise to the chancellorship. He was the only person permitted to address Hitler with the familiar *du*. He was also an indiscreet homosexual.

Röhm was short, stocky, and thick-necked, with a florid countenance. Other descriptions might use the uncomplimentary terms of fat or paunchy. He was born November 28, 1887, in the Bavarian town of Ingolstadt, the son of a railway official. It is either a remarkable coincidence or a curiosity of psychological significance that Hitler, along with almost all of his top henchmen, came

Ernst Röhm

out of a family where the father was domineering and harsh, and Röhm was no exception.

Even from early childhood, Röhm knew he wanted to become a soldier. He realized this ambition when he joined the German Army in 1906. Two years later (around the time Hitler began his tramp days in Vienna), he was a lieutenant. In action during the First World War, he found his niche as an infantry officer and a company commander. He was a combatant devoid of fear who had nothing but contempt for officers or enlisted men who exhibited any sign of cowardice. He was wounded three times, and each time after recovering he returned to the front. A portion of his nose was shot away, and his cheek carried the scar of a bullet, but his fervor was never diminished.

War's end found him with the rank of captain, assigned to District Command VII in München. Contrary to what some of his professional fellow officers thought, he believed that army officers should be political activists; it is difficult to conceive of a more active one than Ernst Röhm. Through his work the army's special intelligence section was formed to maintain a watchful eye over the many political groups that proliferated after the end of hostilities. He eventually replaced Captain Mayr as head of the unit.

After the war a large arsenal was left by the German Army, and Röhm was one of several officers who conspired to divert and cache the arms. The German government had promised the Allies that the guns, ammunition, and vehicles would be dutifully destroyed, and according to the peace treaty, this should have been done. However, in some instances (with the connivance of some Allied officers attached to control commissions), these arms were stored for future use and would later be issued to members of the Freikorps and the SA. As an officer, Röhm had the reputation of a man who resolutely stood by his subordinates, while acting as a buffer between them and his superior officers. For all his dedication as a soldier, he was, paradoxically, a person who casually arranged for the murder of informants who tried to reveal the whereabouts of his hidden arsenals.

It was Röhm—not Hitler—who first stumbled across the German Workers' Party, and it was Röhm who transformed that "talking club" (as one early writer described it) into a viable, fermenting hotbed of activists. It was Röhm who provided the infusion of restless, action-seeking (and action-producing) soldiers and former soldiers, thereby changing the original working-class character of the party. Röhm was already a member when Hitler discovered the party in the fall of 1919. He was impressed with Hitler's oratory, and was instrumental in putting Hitler in touch with politicians and military personnel who could be useful to the party. Without this assistance, it is doubtful that Hitler's political star could have risen so quickly.

The genesis of the SA dates back to the summer of 1920, when Emil Maurice, an ex-convict who later became Hitler's personal chauffeur, was placed in charge of a motley group of unruly party protectors. As a camouflage, in August 1921, they were called the "Gymnastic and Sports Division" of the party, and this transparent attempt to conceal the true purpose of the division was continued until October 1921 when it became known as the SA. Röhm was always the guiding light behind the SA, and it was his influence that brought in the militaristic recruits, his fine hand and expertise that restructured the SA into the formidable force it became in later years. It was Hitler who spouted the words; it was Röhm and his SA who provided the brawn to back them up.

During the latter part of September 1923, Röhm resigned from the Reichswehr and devoted all of his time to Hitler and the cause. Less than two months later he was deeply involved in the Beer Hall Putsch. He was the only leader in the coup d'état who accomplished his objective: to seize the headquarters of the army at the War Ministry in Münich. Two hours after Hitler's march through the streets had been halted and dispersed by police bullets, Röhm realized the futility of the operation, surrendered, and was placed under arrest. He was one of the ten defendants tried for treason. While Hitler was sent to Landsberg Prison, Röhm (although found guilty) was placed on probation and released.

He now entered the most difficult period of his life. While Hitler was serving his sentence, he and Gregor Strasser aligned themselves with the recently formed National Socialist Freedom Movement and won themselves seats in the Reichstag in the May 1924 election. Other than that accomplishment, it was all downhill. During 1924 Röhm endured the embarrassment of having his suitcase and personal papers stolen while he was consorting with questionable acquaintances in a sordid section of Berlin; as a result of this indiscretion, his homosexual proclivities became known to police authorities.

In April 1925 he had a falling-out with Hitler, withdrew from political life, and failed miserably in his efforts to support himself. He drifted about, worked for a short period at a machine factory, became a book salesman, and imposed on his homosexual friends for sustenance. As a civilian, he was totally out of his element. At one time he had frankly acknowledged that "war and unrest appeal to me more than the orderly life of your respectable burgher." But, respectable burgher he was not; virtually destitute, he moved about in the lowest of circles and associated with the dregs of the social stratum. He had also once made the statement that he could "reach an understanding more easily with an enemy soldier than with a German civilian, because the latter is a swine and I don't understand his language." He now found himself living as "a swine."

In 1928 he briefly reconciled with Hitler and traveled throughout Germany renewing contacts with active duty Reichswehr officers as the party chief's envoy. After yet another dispute with Hitler, he abruptly left Germany for South America, accepting the post of military adviser to the Bolivian Army as a lieutenant-colonel. From Bolivia he imprudently sent letters to friends in Germany in which he decried the lack of understanding for homosexuals in that faraway land. Some of the letters addressed to Dr. Karl-Gunther Heimsoth fell into the hands of newspaper journalists and were given widespread publicity.

With Röhm in South America, Hitler placed Captain Franz Pfeffer von Salomon in charge of the SA. This was a move Hitler came to regret, as Pfeffer von Salomon (like Röhm) had an independent mind, but unlike Röhm had no fealty to Hitler, who he characterized as "that flabby Austrian."

By August 1930 Hitler had reached the end of his patience with Pfeffer von Salomon. He relieved him of his command and, on an interim basis, personally assumed leadership of the SA. A telegram was dispatched from München to La Paz, as once again Hitler in a time of need turned to the man who had been so essential to him in past days of travail. By the end of 1930 Röhm had returned to his native Germany, and in January 1931 he was named Chief of Staff of the SA.

He immediately began the task of rebuilding and enlarging the SA, and in so doing brought his homosexual friends into leadership positions. Hitler turned aside all complaints about Röhm's morals, lifestyle, methods, and techniques, and defended the SA by saying it was "not an institute for the moral education of young ladies but a band of tough fighters." And so it was, as the ranks burgeoned to encompass the criminal element as well as sundry undesirables. This was all done with the acquiescence of Hitler, but to the dismay of Reichswehr leaders, who viewed Röhm and his men as distinct threats to displacing the army as the Fatherland's first line of defense. The Treaty of Versailles limited the Reichswehr to a force of 100,000. No such restriction applied to the SA, which operated somewhat like the National Guard in the United States, with many members holding full-time civilian jobs.

With the responsibility of the SA firmly in Röhm's hands, Hitler concentrated on his final push toward his goal. By the time he negotiated his power play to snatch the chancellorship from under the very noses of von Schleicher and von Papen, Röhm had molded the SA into an intimidating strike force. Hitler's private army was ready and eager to be tested. Thanks to Röhm—who had again done his job—Hitler could operate from a position of strength.

While the Nazi Führer was conferring with President von Hindenburg at the Chancellery the morning of January 30, 1933, his entourage huddled expectantly across the square at the Hotel Kaiserhof, like a pack of hovering jackals awaiting distribution of the spoils. Standing vigil at the window with his binoculars trained on the door of the Chancellery stood Ernst Röhm—freebooter, soldier of fortune, renegade from the German officer corps.

The millenium was at hand.

Chapter 4

THE ACE

Hermann Wilhelm Göring was best known as the architect of the Luftwaffe, but, like Röhm, he began his military career in the infantry. He gave the appearance of a genial, bonhomie-type individual who radiated conviviality and good fellowship. He was, in fact, something quite different—a cold, calculating opportunist who trampled anything or anyone who stood in his path. Otto Strasser had this to say about him: "The fat, jolly exterior of this man was a perfect mask for one of the most cruel and unscrupulous characters I have ever met. His was the soul of a butcher."

Once he made it to the top, Göring was the epitome of ostentation. He loved titles, medals, gaudy uniforms,

Hermann Göring

extravagant living, and attention. He would take two wives, and both showered him with slavish devotion.

He was born January 12, 1893, at Rosenheim, in Bavaria. It is ironic that his parents were married in London, a city that reeled from the blows of his bombers in World War II. At the time of his birth his father, a member of the German Consular Service, was working in Haiti. His father was frequently absent from the home because of his official assignments during Hermann's boyhood, and when he retired at the relatively early age of fifty-six, he became a drunk. The result of all this was that young Hermann's godfather, Dr. Ritter Hermann von Epenstein, became his surrogate father—and his mother's surrogate husband. The arrogant von Epenstein (whose father was Jewish) had prestige, money, and influence. He also owned two castles.

Göring received his initial military training at the Cadet School at Karlsruhe after his father and von Epenstein decided he needed the discipline a military school would provide. This was followed by additional instruction at the Prussian Cadet Corps at Lichterfelde. Just in time for the First World War, he became a lieutenant in 1913, attached to the 112th Prinz Wilhelm Infantry Regiment. He became an adjutant in the Second Battalion, experiencing front-line action in several battles, but swelling of his knees caused by rheumatism ended his brief infantry career. He was transferred to a hospital ward at Freiburg, which happened to be the site of an air training school where a friend named Bruno Lörzer was a pilot trainee. He now concluded that infantry warfare was not for him, and he forwarded a written request to his commanding officer asking for a transfer to the flying school. His application for transfer was rejected, and he was ordered to rejoin his unit as soon as he was discharged from the hospital.

Working through his influential godfather, however, he was able to obtain the coveted certificate that stated he was medically unfit for trench duty.

While he was pulling strings right and left, Göring started (without authorization) going aloft with Lieutenant Lörzer as an observer-photographer. Subsequently, pilot Lörzer and ex-infantryman Göring were assigned to the 25th Field Air Detachment of the German Fifth Army in action at the French border. (Lörzer would later become Göring's adviser and Luftwaffe Chief of Personnel.)

In June 1915 Göring was finally admitted to the Freiburg Aviation School, where he excelled in a concentrated period of training. By October he was attached to Jagdstaffel 5, a pursuit squadron on the Western Front. He was to become a skilled pilot, adept at dogfighting, and was given command of his own squadron, Jagdstaffel 27. In May 1918 he recorded his twentieth kill, and was awarded the highly regarded Pour le Merite (the German Victoria Cross), worn as a ribbon around the neck.

On April 21, 1918, Manfred Freiherr von Richthofen, the fabled "Red Knight," was shot down and killed in an air battle with the RAF, bringing to a close a spectacular career in which he registered an impressive eighty victories. Von Richthofen's last will and testament recommended that Captain Wilhelm Reinhardt be promoted to commander of the famous "Flying Circus," and so he was. Less than three months later Reinhardt was killed while testing an experimental Dornier biplane (with Göring looking on from the ground). On July 7, 1918, Lieutenant Hermann Göring was, by direction of the Supreme Commander of the German Armed Forces, appointed commander of the Richthofen Squadron.

Göring now had under his supervision some of the most outstanding aviators of the German Air Force—men like Ernst Udet, Karl Bodenschatz, and a certain young Lieutenant (later Captain) Gehrt, who became a close wartime friend. Udet and Bodenschatz (like Lörzer) would become high-ranking officers in Göring's Luftwaffe. With Gehrt it was to be another story.

When Göring assumed his new command he had no way of knowing that within four months the leaders of the German High Command—General Ludendorff and Field Marshal von Hindenburg—would be asking for a truce. He and his Flying Circus fighter pilots were frustrated and bewildered by the capitulation of the German government at the end of the First World War. In November 1918, he received word that the Kaiser had abdicated, and he was ordered to surrender himself and his men to the nearest Allied forces—the Americans. With military authority in the process of crumbling in all sectors, he chose to ignore the order with the assertion that he would never surrender to the Yanks. There would be another day at the conclusion of another war when he would go out of his way to do just that.

The squadron was eventually disbanded in November at Aschaffenburg near Frankfurt where he delivered an emotional farewell speech to his aviators. The war was over, the Richthofen Flying Circus had passed into history, and Göring was a civilian.

He returned to Münich in full uniform, and had to defend himself in a street attack by resentful Germans who tried to take his medals. He was unprepared for this type of conduct by people he thought he was serving when he repeatedly risked his life on the Western Front. He was also unprepared to undergo the transition to civilian employee. Cast adrift in an alien world, he sought work in the only field in which he had any expertise, and he capitalized on his reputation as a war hero. He had met aircraft designer Anthony Fokker during the war years, and he put this contact to good use. He was hired to represent the Fokker interests as both a salesman and airplane demonstrator in Scandinavia. It was a mutually advantageous arrangement, as Fokker found it to be good business to have his company represented by "the last commander of the famous von Richthofen squadron." Fokker gave him full use of his latest commercial monoplane, the Fokker F7. Göring earned extra money by using the aircraft in his air charter service, flying businessmen around Scandinavia and also making short tourist flights. In addition, he served as an adviser for Danish Airlines.

While in Sweden in 1920 he met an attractive, thirty-two-year-old daughter of an aristocrat who was also a colonel in the Swedish Army. Her name was Karin von Kantzow. She had an eight-year-old son by her husband, from whom she was estranged. Göring began an open liaison with the woman, and they moved into an apartment in Stockholm. Inexplicably, Karin's army captain husband continued to pay her an allowance with which she supported herself and her lover, whose employment record was slowly deteriorating into irregularity. Like Hitler, Röhm, and other future Nazi leaders, he found it quite difficult to function as a civilian in a peace-time economy.

In 1921 Göring returned to Germany, and soon was joined by his Swedish mistress who had obtained a divorce from her patient husband. She and Göring were united in marriage in München on February 3, 1922. With a part of his wife's dowry, the bridegroom purchased a small hunting lodge near München at Bayrischzell, and he enrolled as a student at the University of München. The newlyweds started attending the various political meetings which were being held in München during this period of social upheaval in Germany. It was at one of these gatherings, a mass meeting on the Königsplatz on a Sunday in November 1922, that Göring first saw Adolf Hitler—the man who would completely change the direction of his life.

The chairman of the National Socialist German Workers' Party was present that day, attired in his usual dirty raincoat, but he did not take the platform. Two days later Göring attended one of Hitler's own meetings, heard him speak, and became a convert on the spot. The former commander of the legendary Flying Circus had found his man in the former corporal. The following day he visited Hitler at party headquarters and offered his services. At this point Hitler needed all the help he could get, and, obviously, the membership of a former airman with Göring's reputation was welcomed. It was another example of Hitler's unerring capacity to recognize a good thing when he saw it. He had just the job for the new man—leadership of the SA.

The SA was largely the creation of Ernst Röhm, who was still on active duty with the Reichswehr at this time. The SA, however, lacked the requisite esprit de corps that Hitler had looked for when he placed it under the immediate command of Johann Ulrich Klintsch, who would now be replaced by Göring. The SA became Göring's main project. He drilled them relentlessly, introducing a sense of discipline previously unknown to the men, who were essentially rowdy street brawlers. In an effort to upgrade the ranks and inspire a sense of élan, he brought along some of his former flying friends, including his comrade Gehrt.

In November 1923 Göring became enmeshed in the planning of the Beer Hall Putsch (so called because of events that occurred in a beer hall the night before the disastrous march through the streets of Münich). On the evening of November 8, Hitler—with Göring at his side—

made a dramatic entrance into the Burgerbraukeller, one of Münich's largest beer halls, and interrupted a speech by the Bavarian State Commissioner, Gustav von Kahr. Hitler pulled a pistol and fired a shot into the ceiling to get the crowd's attention, and then at virtual gunpoint attempted to coerce von Kahr and his associates into joining the Nazis in an overthrow of the Bavarian state government. With Hitler waving a Browning under his nose, von Kahr agreed to the demands. Göring was in charge of the SA that night, and it was his assignment to maintain strict control over the assemblage. At evening's end Hitler and Göring congratulated themselves for a job well done, but the next morning they discovered to their consternation that von Kahr (once he was away from the gun-wielding Hitler) had repudiated his "agreement" and had taken steps to quell the uprising.

The effectiveness of von Kahr's measures became apparent the next day. During the armed confrontation with the police, Göring took a bullet in the thigh and fell to the pavement as the Nazi insurgents were routed. He was helped into a nearby house by two Jewish women who bathed his wound, applied bandages, and harbored him until nightfall. He managed to avoid arrest, and headed toward Austria. At the border, however, his passport was confiscated and he was taken into custody, then transported to a hospital at Garmisch. Based on his promise not to attempt further escape, he was permitted to remain in the hospital instead of in jail. Despite his "word of honor," he immediately slipped across the border to freedom, wearing a fur coat over his hospital night shirt with a false passport furnished by friends.

With the aid of his wife, Göring made it to a Catholic hospital in Innsbruck where he underwent surgery. Infection set in, and the physicians started injecting morphine to alleviate the pain, the beginning of his long addiction to morphine. With Hitler in jail awaiting trial, he remained hospitalized and was visited regularly by Hitler's sister, Paula, as well as sundry party emissaries. His house, car, and bank account were impounded by Bavarian authorities to further complicate his problems. He was discharged from the hospital just before Christmas, a penniless fugitive from justice. He had no source of income whatsoever, and was dependent on his in-laws for food and money, which they generously provided.

By February 1924 he had recovered from his gunshot wound, but he despaired because of his physical weakness and sexual impotency, and his use of morphine did not abate. He began to associate with local agitators, and from his sanctuary in Austria he bitterly attacked the German authorities for having the audacity to impose a prison term on his leader. Austria took a dim view of these fulminations, and invited him to take leave of their country.

Accepting Italy's offer of asylum, Göring and his wife (who had become a Hitler follower herself) proceeded to Venice in April 1924, and then on to Rome where he had an audience with Benito Mussolini, the fascist dictator, who declined his request for a two million-lire loan to the Nazi Party. The Görings' fortunes continued at a low ebb, and in April 1925 Karin visited Hitler in Münich to ask for financial assistance for her husband. She was given a small amount of money and an autographed picture of the Führer.

The following month the destitute couple wandered back to Stockholm where they were taken in by Karin's parents. Göring degenerated into a physical and mental wreck, and was hospitalized for observation and treatment. When denied drugs, he became violent and attacked a nurse, and as a consequence was restrained in a straitjacket. After further examination, he was certified insane and moved to Langbro Asylum for the Insane on September 1, 1925, where he remained for six months.

While Göring was in Sweden, much had happened in Germany. Hitler was released from Landsberg Prison in December 1924, and then retreated to Berchtesgaden. Gregor Strasser was beginning to flex his political muscles. In 1925 Field Marshal Paul von Hindenburg was elected President. And the Reichstag had voted to grant amnesty to political exiles—and this included Hermann Göring.

In October 1927 he returned to his native Germany. It was not until early 1928 that his wife could join him in Berlin, due to health problems. He was anxious to resume his active participation in party affairs, but all important posts had been filled during his involuntary absence. At a meeting at the Sans Souci Hotel, Hitler suggested to him that he become a candidate for the Reichstag on the Nazi ticket. He did not have to be asked twice.

When the Nazi Party seated twelve deputies in the Reichstag in the elections of May 20, 1928, Göring was one of them. He thus gained entrée to a parliamentary body he would help destroy. Now that he was a member of the Reichstag, he was entitled to a free railway pass and 800 marks a month, plus expenses. With the prestige of being a duly elected official, he resumed his contacts with executives connected with the German aircraft industry, and this in turn placed him in association with other industrialists, as well as bankers. He soon augmented his income with 1,000 marks a month as lobbyist for Lufthansa Airlines. There were frequent lunches and dinners at the Göring flat at which time he entertained potential contributors to the Nazi treasury. He was invaluable to Hitler in this respect, because of all the top Nazis—

other than the minimally accomplished Hess—he was the only one versed in the social graces. He knew how to charm people.

It was Göring who arranged a small party on New Year's Day in 1931, attended by, among others, Hitler, industrialist Fritz Thyssen, and Hjalmar Schacht, president of the Reichsbank. Hitler talked for two hours, outlining his remedy for Germany's ills: rearmament and public works projects. He said nothing about killing anyone who disagreed with him. When questions were raised about the disturbing activities of the SA, host Göring reassured one and all that the unruly elements would be restrained, and that once the Nazi Party had the support of the apprehensive bankers and industrialists, the objectives of the party would be achieved in a legal and proper manner.

When Gregor Strasser found out about the meeting in Göring's flat, he protested that Hitler was "selling out to big money interests" and straying from the principles and goals of National Socialism. But Hitler, playing all angles, was satisfied. He was now reaping dividends from all sources.

During 1931, Karin Göring, in ill health for years, began to grow weaker. Her mother died in September, and despite her frail condition, Karin returned to Sweden for the funeral. Within a month she joined her mother in death. After his wife's funeral, Göring returned to Berlin and, following a brief stay at the Kaiserhof Hotel, he moved into a flat in the Kaiserdamm. He now threw himself into political activity with even more intensity, as Hitler began his unsuccessful attempt to dislodge von Hindenburg as president of Germany. There is some suspicion that Göring was again using morphine at this time. He constantly talked about his deceased wife, but this did not prevent him from striking up a close relationship with a tall, blond stage actress named Emmy Sonnemann who would soon share his flat.

In the July 1932 elections, the Nazis became the strongest party in the Reichstag with 230 seats, and as a result of this strength Göring became president of the Reichstag on August 20. The man who seven years before had been confined to an institution for the mentally ill in Sweden was now in a position equivalent to the Speaker of the House of Representatives in the United States. Franz von Papen was chancellor. But Adolf Hitler and the Nazis were circling and closing in.

As everything started dovetailing the evening of January 29, 1933, Göring telephoned Emmy Sonnemann in Weimar where she was performing in a stage play. Anticipating a triumphant morrow, he asked her to join him in Berlin for the celebration, and she did so.

On the evening of January 30 the new chancellor stood on the balcony of the Chancellery as the SA passed by in review, carrying flaming torches. Clad in the uniform of an SA leader, Göring was inside delivering a message by radio to the German people. He told them to expect "honor and freedom for the nation."

He could not have selected more inappropriate words to describe what was in store for his radio audience.

Chapter 5

THE PROPAGANDIST

One of Hitler's most consistent and forceful advocates of violence and warfare was himself a lifelong noncombatant. He was Paul Joseph Göbbels, born October 29, 1897, in Rheydt, a textile center in the Rhineland, the offspring of working-class parents of little education. He was an unlikely type of person to find a place in the Nazi firmament. He was diminutive—almost dwarfish—in appearance, and crippled. Even as an adult he was just over five feet tall, and his weight barely exceeded one hundred pounds. Searing brown eyes set in lean features made him look more Celtic than German.

At the age of four, he was afflicted with poliomyelitis which retarded his growth and, as a result of surgery, shortened his left leg so as to leave him with a permanent

Paul Joseph Göbbels

limp. His parents were devout Catholics, and at one time nurtured the hope that their physically handicapped son would enter the priesthood. His father was a stern man, employed as a supervisor in a textile factory. His mother, of Dutch origin, frequently took the smallish boy to church to pray for his health and recovery. As a child, he became a semi-recluse in his attic room, reading voraciously. When the First World War began in 1914, he was but sixteen years old and, not unexpectedly, rejected for military service. The man who would one day be termed the "intellectual of the Nazi Party" proved himself to be an outstanding student in high school, although even as a teenager he displayed a supercilious manner that did not endear him to his classmates.

He started his higher education in 1917 by enrolling for one term at Bonn University. He then applied for and received a series of interest-free loans from the Albertus Magnus Society, a Catholic charitable organization, which enabled him to further pursue his university studies. In several letters to the society he represented himself as an impoverished student and beseeched the Diocesan Committee to favor him with financial assistance. (It took legal persuasion in 1930 on the part of the society to extract repayment from the thankless applicant, who by then had become anti-Catholic.)

After his term at Bonn, Göbbels became somewhat of a scholastic vagabond. In 1918 he attended the University of Freiburg, and then on to Wurzburg University. After the Armistice he moved to the University of München in 1919, and then in 1920 he ended up at the University of Heidelberg where he took his doctorate in philosophy in 1921 at the age of twenty-four.

After the insulation of academia, his initial excursion into the real world was a humbling experience for the graduate, who fancied himself a man of letters. He wrote a short novel, which was rejected by a publisher; a play that he had written met the same fate. He returned to his hometown of Rheydt and continued his writing, but all of his literary submissions were rejected by publishers. He finally landed a clerical job at a bank in Cologne, through the assistance of a girlfriend who feared he was becoming suicidal. She had become alarmed by his frustration, depression, and moodiness.

He still considered himself a writer, and on January 23, 1924, he sent a letter of application (falsifying his employment history) to the *Berlin Tageblatt*, a daily newspaper, requesting a job on the editorial staff. He was not hired, nor were the numerous articles he submitted accepted. With no success whatsoever in the literary field, Göbbels made several attempts to gain a foothold in the theater in any capacity available (actor, director, stage manager, or writer). Rebuffed at every turn, his efforts in this direction were no more successful than his writing endeavors.

It was in the year 1924, while again in the ranks of the unemployed, that his interest in politics became serious and his attraction to Hitler and the Nazi Party intensified. His first job in the political arena was secretary to a Reichstag deputy named Franz von Wiegershaus, who represented the Popular Liberty Party, and this provided the eventual opening through which he slipped into the Nazi sphere. In 1925 he was hired by Gregor and Otto Strasser, replacing Heinrich Himmler on their payroll. He was given secretarial tasks, with additional duties as an editorial assistant. Göbbels was now a Nazi.

The primary organ of the Strasser faction was the *Berliner Arbeiterzeitung*, with Otto the editor, but they also published several periodicals, one of which was the

Nazionalsozialistische Briefe. Göbbels was given the collateral job as editor of the *Briefe.* There was no question that the Strassers and Hitler were on a collision course. The only uncertainty was: Who would win? While in the employ of the Strassers, Göbbels became their spokesman, in both verbal and written expression. He began to capitalize on his latent public speaking talents as a party mouthpiece when he was not pursuing various young women. He was to establish quite a reputation as a philanderer.

The stunted Rhinelander had by this time forsaken his Catholic faith, to the disappointment of his mother and father who regarded him as an apostate, although this did not deter him from writing home for money when his finances were periodically exhausted. He first met Hitler in late 1925 in Elberfield, at which time he was introduced as Gregor Strasser's secretary. He meticulously maintained a diary which has survived, and during these months the entries reflect numerous complimentary passages on the Strassers, with concomitant criticisms of Hitler. When Hitler decided to woo him from the Strasser fold, this would all change—drastically.

Over a span of several months Hitler began to flatter Göbbels with attention until he succumbed to the master blandisher and made the decision to change horses. In February 1926 he abandoned the Strassers. He was now a Hitler man.

The transference of fidelity opened up an entirely new and fascinating world to him and he started to spend a great deal of time with his new Pied Piper. Whereas he previously espoused the Strasser line, he now was the voice of Hitler, in whose shadow he became the consummate sycophant. His diary suddenly filled with effusive praise of his new leader, whom he now called "a

genius" and "the creative instrument of Fate and Deity."
He described a Hitler speech in these words: "At first he
spoke hesitantly and timidly as though he was searching
for the right words to formulate his ambitious thoughts.
Then, suddenly, his speech picked up momentum. I was
seized. I listened. The crowd started to stir. I became al-
ternately hot and cold. A flame went though me. This was
a command. At that moment I was reborn. Now I knew
which path to take!"

In October 1926 Göbbels was rewarded with the appointment of Gauleiter (District Leader) of Berlin. Thus,
he returned to the bailiwick of the Strassers. When he arrived at the Berlin railway station (alighting from a third-
class compartment), he was met by his former employer,
Otto, who was still trying to work within the party structure. Göbbels moved into Berlin at a crucial juncture, for
it was during this period that Hitler was consolidating his
party strength and planning a political beachhead—a
breakthrough to Nazi membership in the Reichstag.

In July 1927 Göbbels acquired another weapon when
his own newspaper, *Der Angriff* (The Attack), appeared on
the streets to rival the Strasser publications. The battle
lines were being drawn. When the Nazis put twelve
deputies in the Reichstag in 1928, Göbbels was one of
them. In November 1928 Hitler appointed him head of
party propaganda, replacing Gregor Strasser. It was an
apprenticeship for a post of far-reaching influence that
was just beyond the horizon. In 1930 it was Gauleiter
Göbbels—on Hitler's orders—who formally expelled the
recalcitrant Otto Strasser from the party. Göbbels was
now in while Otto was out.

On December 12, 1931, Göbbels married Magda
Quandt, a well-to-do divorcee who was living luxuriously

in a Berlin flat on a monthly allowance of 4,000 marks, supplied by her ex-husband, a wealthy industrialist. As was his custom, Hitler was present at the ceremony as the perennial best man. After the marriage the bridegroom moved out of his two-room apartment into his bride's spacious accommodation on the Reichskanzlerplatz, where Hitler would be a frequent guest in the following months. With the death of Karin Göring on October 17, 1931, Hitler transferred his social base to the Göbbelses' residence where he repaired for meals and relaxation.

When Hitler decided to challenge von Hindenburg for the presidency, it was Göbbels who announced the candidacy before a packed house at the Berlin Sportpalast in February 1932. He joined Hitler, Göring, and Gregor Strasser on the speaking circuit, advancing the Hitler campaign platform: something for everybody. In his zeal to ingratiate himself with his idol, he intemperately assailed von Hindenburg on the floor of the Reichstag, and as a result of his insulting outburst was temporarily excluded from the chamber. The election was the first real test of Göbbels's propaganda machine. The election was lost, but the machine was not. The device would be refined and expanded to operate with frightening efficiency in years to come. Once again, Hitler had chosen the right man for the right job at the right time.

On the night before Hitler's appointment to the chancellorship, there was a celebration at the Göbbelses' flat, located in one of Berlin's best residential neighborhoods. As Magda Göbbels served sweets to the rejoicing guests, her husband dramatically clasped hands with Hitler and Göring to form an ecstatic circle. He had come a long way since his days of rejection, despair, and deprivation. The doctor of philosophy whose parents hoped would become a man of the cloth had found his Messiah in the mesmeric Adolf Hitler, to whom he was attracted like a moth to flame—with the same results.

Chapter 6

THE DEPUTY

Of all the members of the Third Reich's top echelon, Rudolf Hess was the most enigmatic. He was sometimes termed "the conscience of the party," but when it came to promoting Hitler and the Nazis, he was never fettered with constraints of ethics, social niceties, or conscience. An early Nazi Party member named Kurt Ludecke gave this impression of him: "A man sat in front of me who was not easy to fathom . . . Hess made me feel uneasy. I could not place him and he did nothing to meet me halfway. He was polite, too polite, very aloof. I could not break through his armor." Very few people could. Hess was born April 26, 1894, in Alexandria, Egypt, where his German father was in the export business. Like so many of the men who would form the nucleus of Hitler's hierarchy, he came

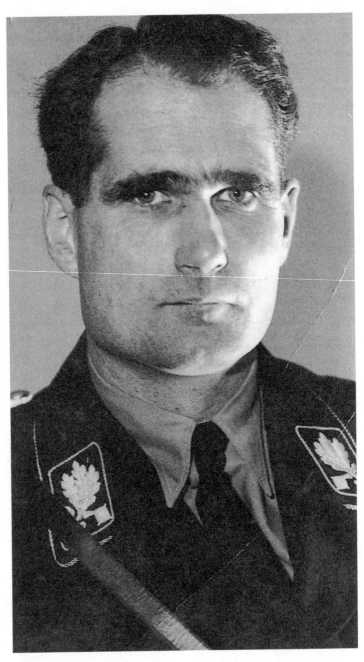

Rudolf Hess

from a home situation where the father was a stern disciplinarian.

At the age of fourteen, young Rudolf was sent to Germany to complete his education, in Godesberg. He was always a good student, and hoped to eventually matriculate at Oxford. In adulthood, he was tall, slender, and athletic, with bushy eyebrows, a grim-visage, and dark hair over an angular face. He almost looked like an Irishman. After completing school in 1912, he worked as an apprentice for an export business in Hamburg before volunteering for military service in the First Bavarian Infantry Regiment as World War I commenced. This development ended his dream of an Oxford education.

He was wounded in combat, and, after convalescence, commissioned as a lieutenant. He also served in the so-called List Regiment, which had an officer's runner named Adolf Hitler. In 1918 he volunteered to join the Imperial Flying Corps, finishing his instruction in October of that year. He was released from active duty on December 13, 1918. His military aerial career was cut short by the Armistice, but his pilot training would be put to good use some twenty-three years later.

Former soldiers were exempt from the prerequisite of entrance examinations at German universities after the war, and Hess enrolled as a student at Münich University in 1920. One of his courses was economics, taken at the insistence of his father, who was still putting pressure on him and who still harbored the faint hope that his son would be a success in the business world. Instead, like so many of the returning ex-servicemen, he took to fighting in the streets as a member of the Freikorps, the volunteer quasi-military organization established to resist the steadily increasing influence of the Communists. He also began speaking at various rallies and joined the Thule Society, an anti-Semitic group.

In April 1920 Hess joined the National Socialist German Workers' Party. It did not take long for him to fall under Hitler's spell. He became a member of the SA, a confidant to Hitler, and even in those early years pursuant to Hitler's wishes, began the practice of compiling a confidential index-card file on friend and foe alike.

He was totally involved in Hitler's unsuccessful Beer Hall Putsch in November 1923. As Hitler led the street march in Münich, Hess held two unsympathetic ministers hostage at a hideout in the mountains near the Tegernsee. When the coup disintegrated into a rout, the news reached Hess and his captives. Hess released the ministers and slipped across the border into Austria to avoid apprehension. He later returned, was given a relatively light sentence of eighteen months for his participation in the operation, and joined Hitler in confinement at Landsberg Prison.

He used his time at Landsberg to help Hitler in the composition and formation of ideas projected in *Mein Kampf*, and it was during this period that he became thoroughly entrenched with the future chancellor. Oddly, while Hitler was rethinking his strategy and altering his game plan from violent overthrow to legal assumption of office, Hess was postulating something else. A visitor who was at the prison to talk to both of the comfortably housed inmates wrote that Hess repeatedly remarked: "We must learn to be much more brutal in our methods. That is the only way to deal with our enemies."

After their release from prison—Hess was freed ten days after his leader—Hess became Hitler's secretary and virtual shadow, frequently accompanying him on official party matters. As secretary, he would screen visitors before they were permitted an audience with the Führer. One of the first female members of the Nazi Party was Ilse Prohl.

She had initially met Hess in 1920, but it wasn't until December 1927 that she became his wife, with Hitler a witness at the wedding.

Until Göring's reentry upon the scene in 1928, Hitler had to rely on Hess to represent him in personal contacts that necessitated some degree of social finesse or sophistication, which was not exactly Hitler's forté. It was Hess, for instance, who in 1928 arranged through banker Fritz Thyssen the funds to purchase the posh Barlow Palace at 45 Briennerstraße, overlooking the Königsplatz in München, which was remodeled and converted into the "Brown House" party headquarters. When the Nazis assumed occupancy in 1931, Hitler mounted a portrait of himself on a wall with the caption: "Nothing happens in this movement except what I wish." It was not only a statement but also a warning to anyone who entertained ideas of independent action, as many unsuspecting citizens would soon realize. Although an integral cog in the early party power machine, the introverted and ascetic Hess always seemed to be in the background, and his very closeness to the leader hindered his emergence as a separate, distinct personality apart from his Nazi contemporaries.

It was not until mid-December 1932 that Hitler rewarded Hess's loyalty by moving him out of the secretary's anonymity to a position of broader responsibility. His new job was to oversee and control the party's political activities in all sectors of Germany. The rudimentary index-card intelligence system he devised and instituted in the early 1920s at Hitler's behest had by now evolved into an elaborate source of confidential information. It would soon be utilized.

Heinrich Himmler

Chapter 7

THE ENFORCER

As Hitler's tyranny enveloped Germany and then relentlessly crept across Europe, the man who unemotionally implemented the policy of repression and extermination of lives was Heinrich Himmler. Himmler's function was to impose Hitler's will upon others and incarcerate or kill those who offered resistance to his leadership. Hitler set the rules, and Himmler enforced them. Adolf Eichmann. Klaus Barbie. Dr. Josef Mengele. These names are equated with limitless cruelty and murder. But they were all underlings. Their boss—the death master at the top of the ladder—was Himmler. Hitler couldn't have chosen a better man for the job.

Himmler was, in effect, the Führer's chief of police. He was given immense power which he never hesitated to use. His domain included the Gestapo, the SS, and the dreaded concentration camps. His jurisdiction extended to every corner of Germany and to every inch of territory absorbed by military conquest.

Paradoxically, Himmler's appearance was disarming, as reflected in the delineation offered by Major-General Walter Dornberger, who at one time was in charge of the German rocket center at Peenemunde:

> He looked to me like an intelligent elementary schoolteacher, certainly not a man of violence. I could not for the life of me see anything outstanding or extraordinary about the middle-sized, youthfully slender man in his gray SS uniform. Under a brow of average height two gray-blue eyes looked out at me, behind a glittering pince-nez, with an air of peaceful interrogation. The trimmed moustache below the straight, well-shaped nose traced a dark line on his unhealthy, pale features. The lips were colorless and very thin. Only the inconspicuous, receding chin surprised me. The skin of his neck was flaccid and wrinkled. With a broadening of his constant, set smile, faintly mocking and sometimes contemptuous about the corners of his mouth, two rows of excellent white teeth appeared between the thin lips. His slender, pale, and almost girlish soft hands, covered with blue veins, lay motionless on the table throughout the conversation.

Himmler was born in Münich on October 7, 1900, the second son of an authoritarian schoolmaster. As a boy, he yearned to be a soldier. He volunteered for military service in 1917, serving in the 11th Bavarian Infantry Regiment, training in Regensburg. He attended an officer-cadet school in Freising in 1918, but the end of the war terminated his bid to become an officer. Following his discharge from the army on December 18, 1918, he drifted toward Berlin, where he worked briefly for a brush merchant before finding employment in a glue factory.

Although the original police reports and court dockets have been destroyed, diligent researchers have pieced together a period of Himmler's early life he later tried to erase. Like Röhm, there was an interlude during which he associated with the basest levels of the Berlin community. Unlike Röhm, however, his interests were heterosexual.

According to a police report dated April 2, 1919, prepared by Berlin Police Inspector Franz Stirmann who was attached to Police Station No. 456 of the Spissenstraße Precinct, Himmler resided in a house of prostitution at No. 45 Acherstraße in the Moabit district. The future Reichsführer-SS shared living quarters with his girlfriend, a prostitute named Frieda Wagner, seven years his elder, who partially supported him. He suddenly disappeared from the Berlin scene in early 1920, about the time authorities found the woman's murdered body. The police located Himmler in Münich and arrested him on July 4, 1920. He returned to the capital to face homicide charges in the Berlin-Brandenburg Criminal Police Court. The eventual verdict was not guilty, but inasmuch as the court records no longer exist, the reason for and circumstances of the acquittal remain a mystery.

During these early years he also studied agriculture, and began work as an apprentice in the small town of Ingolstadt (Röhm's birthplace). In August 1922 he was awarded his agricultural diploma from the University of Münich's Technical College, which led to employment as a laboratory assistant for a fertilizer company in a small community near Münich.

A year later, in August 1923, he applied for membership in the Nazi Party. He had begun to develop anti-Semitic tendencies even before he graduated from the university, and it is obvious that he was comfortable within the Nazi framework. As a party neophyte, he had a minor role in the Beer Hall Putsch in November 1923, which turned into a fiasco with the conviction and imprisonment of Hitler and Hess, and the ignominious flight of the wounded Göring. While the party stalwarts marched down the streets, Himmler was with Röhm at the War Ministry, standing behind a barbed wire fence and clutching a flag. Apparently Himmler's employer took a dim view of their newly hired lab assistant being actively engaged in efforts to overthrow the Bavarian government, and he was fired.

Unemployed and restless, he returned to his parents' home in Münich. He incurred the wrath of his family by declining to seek employment. He explained that he needed the time to involve himself in "politics," and he began appearing as a speaker for anti-Semitic groups in Bavaria. In August 1925 he rejoined the Nazi Party. Hitler, who had been released from prison in December 1924, and the Strasser brothers were in the process of reconstructing the party, and Himmler was hired by the Strassers. He became Gregor Strasser's secretary and deputy, and worked in Bavaria as his district organizer. The Strassers would rue the day they brought Himmler into the fold.

In 1925 Himmler also joined the *Schutzstaffel* (Protective Guard), or SS, and was assigned SS Number 168. The SS was initially formed by Hitler in 1923 as his personal bodyguard force, with Josef Berchtold as the head. Berchtold was eventually supplanted by Erhard Heiden, and Himmler was to be rewarded by Hitler with the appointment as Heiden's deputy and second-in-command. Like

Göbbels, Himmler had now shifted from the Strasser camp to the Hitler camp.

In 1927 he became romantically involved with Margarete "Marga" Concerzowo, a nurse of Polish background who owned a nursing home in Berlin. Like Frieda Wagner, she was seven years older than Himmler. They married in July 1928, and with the money Marga realized from the sale of her nursing home, the newlyweds purchased a modest chicken farm at Waldtrudering, near Münich, to augment his meager income. That same year, they had a daughter, Gudrun, but it was not a happy union, and to compound problems the poultry farm was not a resounding success. In a 1929 letter to her absent husband in Berlin, Marga complained bitterly: "The chickens are laying terribly poorly, only two eggs a day. I am furious; how are we supposed to live on that and then even save for Whitsunday. Always bad luck. Always more money problems." But Himmler had more pressing responsibilities in Berlin, and selling eggs was not one of his priorities.

On January 8, 1929, Hitler named him Reichsführer of the SS, replacing Heiden. Although the twenty-eight-year-old former agronomy student now had a job beyond his fondest expectations, far more power would soon be his. Within a few eventful years his name would strike terror in the hearts of millions as he climbed the ladder Hitler placed before him. When Himmler assumed command of the SS, the force totaled 280 men, and was a subordinate unit within the SA. He assiduously started expanding the rolls of the black-uniformed SS, and his influence did not take long to surface. He issued a "Marriage Code" for the members that required prospective benedicts and fiancees to obtain a certificate of racial purity before the wedding could be sanctioned. The certificate was issued by the SS. The man who was promulgating marital guidelines for SS members was himself a less than exemplary husband to his wife or father to his daughter Gudrun. While separated from his wife he acquired a mistress who bore him two children, resulting in additional pecuniary burdens on his strained resources.

Himmler became a member of the Reichstag in 1930, but—unlike Göring and Göbbels—his presence in that chamber was not as a legislator or serious activist. He was there primarily as a rubber stamp to cast a vote along strict party lines. His interests lay elsewhere.

In June 1931 he hired an ex-naval officer named Reinhard Heydrich to take charge of the new Security Service of the SS (*Sicherheitsdienst*, or SD). The Himmler/Heydrich tandem would mean the end of human rights in Germany.

By April 1932 the SS membership had swelled to 30,000, and although still a part of the SA, it was beginning to operate as a counterbalance to the parent organization. Hitler was becoming wary of the SA and his uncertainty of their allegiance worried him. What he wanted was the development of an elite, disciplined, paramilitary force of loyalists dedicated to him personally. This was the task he entrusted to Himmler when he replaced Heiden.

Röhm was in South America with the Bolivian Army during this time, and Himmler on more than one occasion corresponded with him in a cordial manner. When Röhm returned to Germany and became chief of staff of the SA in January 1931, under the existing table of organization Himmler was nominally under the supervision of the former Reichswehr captain. Hitler was not ready to alter this sensitive arrangement, but he employed his usual divide-and-conquer technique by investing the SS chief with other responsibilities independent of Röhm. In the final reckoning, there would be no doubt as to where Himmler stood.

Reinhard Heydrich

Chapter 8

THE HANGMAN

When Reinhard Tristan Eugen Heydrich sought entry into the ranks of the SA, he was without a job and did not have any visible means of support—he was at rock bottom. Within a mere three years he was in an official position, making decisions as to which of his countrymen should die and which should live. Such was the remarkable turn-about in the life of the man who would earn the fearsome sobriquet "the Hangman."

Heydrich was born March 7, 1904, in Halle, where his father (a former opera singer) owned and operated a music academy. He became an accomplished violinist, but his musical proclivities did not prevent him from joining the Freikorps at the early age of sixteen. He was an athletic type, and developed into an adept fencer. He completed his high school education in 1922, and, rather than pursuing a musical career, he entered the German Naval Academy in Kiel that same year. He did not seem to be very popular with his fellow cadets, who spurned him and regarded him as somewhat of a misfit. Despite his problems with his comrades at the academy, he received training in wireless telegraphy and signals, graduated, and received a commission as a lieutenant in radio intelligence.

In 1931 he became involved with the daughter of an influential industrialist, allegedly impregnating her: he then broke his promise to marry her by announcing his engagement to another girl, Lina von Osten (his future wife). He was suspended from duty and required to appear before a naval board. After hearing the evidence (including Heydrich's testimony in which he tried to place blame on the girl), the board concluded that he did not measure up to the standards expected of a German naval officer, and ordered him dismissed. His nine-year naval career was over. He returned to his hometown of Halle in disgrace, dishonorably discharged.

The loss of uniform and prestige had a jolting effect on the twenty-seven-year-old Heydrich, who had been cutting quite a swath with impressionable young women. An attempt to find a suitable job with the Merchant Marine was unsuccessful. Unemployed, and unable to adjust to his sudden change to civilian status, he floundered about and ultimately made application for an executive position with the SA, citing his naval experience as qualification. His application was routed to the desk of Ernst Röhm, who apparently was not interested in acquiring the services of the cashiered naval officer. Röhm made the mistake of forwarding the application to Himmler, who at this propitious time was looking for a man to run *Sicherheitsdienst* (SD), his new SS Security Service.

Although Heydrich did not actually have any intelligence experience, Himmler was impressed by the résumé and attached photograph, and favored the job-hungry applicant with a personal interview on June 4, 1931. The meeting was held at an unlikely place: Himmler's chicken ranch at Waldtrudering, where the Reichsführer-SS was recuperating from a bout with the flu. Himmler was even more impressed when he roused himself out of bed and came face to face with the tall, lithe ex-naval lieutenant. Although he himself did not fit into the mold, Himmler wanted to recruit into the SS the very specimen exemplified by the blond-haired, blue-eyed, classic Nordic-type who now stood before him. In appearance, he was everything Himmler wasn't.

As a consequence of this interview, during which the uneasy applicant was requested to write down his conception of a security or intelligence service, Heydrich was hired on the spot. He moved to Münich where he rented a room at 23 Turkenstraße. On August 10, 1931, with the rank of Sturmführer-SS (equivalent to his former grade of naval lieutenant), he reported for work at the Brown House on the Briennerstraße where he was given a personal tour of the premises by Himmler. He was assigned a tiny office which he had to share with a low-level adjutant. While exploring the building, he noticed that in another room a nondescript clerk named Martin Bormann sat working at an old kitchen table used as a desk.

The meteoric rise of Heydrich was about to start. He soon developed a friendly working relationship with Rudolf Hess, who directed party affairs from his Brown House office. On December 26, 1931, he married his fiancee, Lina von Osten, a dedicated Nazi who rivaled him when it came to anti-Semitism. In July 1932 he was promoted to Standartenführer-SS (full colonel), and given the title of Chief of the SD, which he tried to pattern after the British Secret Service. Heydrich and his wife moved to a rented house at 4 Zuccali Street in Münich, which also doubled as a second headquarters for the SD. His responsibilities were not limited to the SD, however. He became Himmler's valued chief of staff, and in this role helped develop the entire SS. He was now Himmler's right-hand man. Hitler set the goals. Himmler decided how the SS and the SD could help achieve those goals. Heydrich did it.

The two-headed dragon that was the SA had now grown a third head. The SD (under Heydrich) was a part of the SS (under Himmler) which was a part of the SA (under Röhm). With his new position, Heydrich had regained his prestige and uniform, but not remuneration; SS officers were not generously paid in 1932, and their money woes would not abate until the Nazis came to power. They did not have to wait long.

Chapter 9

THE BUREAUCRAT

Among the Nazi power brokers there was mutual distrust, resentment, jealousy, and incessant infighting as each tried to enhance his own fief. But there was unanimity on one particular: They all hated Martin Bormann. The object of this disaffection was born on June 17, 1900, in Halberstadt, the son of a postal clerk who had been a trumpeter in a military band. He was four years old when his father died. His mother remarried, and young Martin found himself with a banker as his stepfather.

Bormann was drafted into the army as the First World War was grinding to a close, and was discharged from the service after eight months without combat duty. He then began working in farm management for a livelihood. In 1922 he joined the Freikorps, becoming treasurer of his

Martin Bormann

group, and was soon implicated in a political murder. He was arrested in July 1923 in Leipzig, and in 1924 convicted as an accomplice in the homicide, for which he was imprisoned for a term of one year. After his release from prison, he briefly returned to his former type of employment, maintaining records on small farmers who rented the land they cultivated. In 1927 he became a member of the Nazi Party, in which his initial job was as a junior press officer in Thuringia. He subsequently held a variety of minor positions in party offices that utilized his affinity for working with funds and ledgers.

In 1928 he met Gerda Buch, the daughter of Major Walter Buch, a former Prussian Army officer who acted as the party's disciplinarian. Like Heydrich's wife, Gerda was as passionately pro-Hitler as she was anti-Semitic. Bormann's career was given a boost the following year when they were united in marriage, with Hitler a witness in the ceremony. One of the bridesmaids was Hitler's young niece, Angela "Geli" Raubal, who would figure prominently in Bormann's rise from obscurity.

The ambitious Bormann became a staff officer of the SA under Captain Franz Pfeffer von Salomon, but lost that job when Röhm took over the leadership of the Brown Shirts in January 1931 and brought in his own cadre of assistants. Bormann, who always seemed to be working with money and figures, was placed in control of funds with which he paid medical bills and—significantly— extended loans to party members. He eventually became the party's disbursing officer, or official paymaster. He was the person who held the keys to the party treasury, so to speak, and arranged the distribution of the largesse so that many top party officials became indebted to him. It didn't take long for the canny Bormann to recognize the importance of these political IOUs.

It was no coincidence that Bormann's real influence began about the time of Geli Raubal's death under peculiar circumstances during the 1931 Oktoberfest. Bormann had provided rent out of party funds for the luxury apartment Geli shared with Hitler at 26 Prinzregentenplatz in Münich. Despite the nineteen-year disparity in their ages, Hitler had become enamored of his half-sister's provocative daughter in a bizarre liaison with overtones of sexual aberration, whose precise term would be coprophilia. The fun-loving Geli wanted to continue her singing lessons; Hitler disapproved. He became insanely jealous of her, and forbade her to see other men, although this did not inhibit her from having affairs with Hitler's former bodyguard (Emil Maurice) and a Jewish artist. While Hitler expected his niece to be faithful to him, it was an entirely different story when it involved his own conduct, as he—surreptitiously—was beginning a relationship with Eva Braun, who was even younger than Geli.

The strange six-year affair with the strong-willed niece culminated in a violent quarrel with her possessive uncle on the afternoon of September 18, 1931. The following morning she was found dead on the floor of her room, shot near the heart, with Hitler's 6.35-caliber Walther pistol next to her body. When housekeeper Anni Winter could not gain entrance to Geli's locked room, she telephoned Rudolf Hess at the Brown House; shortly thereafter, Hess and Gregor Strasser arrived and broke down the door to discover the dead young woman. According to some acquaintances who were close to the situation, the twenty-three-year-old Geli was pregnant at the time of her death, which was officially ruled a suicide. It was the ever-efficient Martin Bormann who stepped into the breach and arranged with authorities for the body to be transported in a sealed coffin to Vienna, where she

Geli Raubal

was buried at Central Cemetery. The services were conducted by a Catholic priest, Father Johann Pant, who later said: "They pretended that she committed suicide; I should never have allowed a suicide to be buried in consecrated ground. From the fact that I gave her Christian burial you can draw your own conclusions, which I cannot communicate to you."

There were conflicting accounts of Hitler's whereabouts on the evening of September 18. He claimed to have been in Nuremberg, but this was refuted by Herr Karl Zehntner, proprietor of the Bratwurstglöckl, the Münich tavern at 9 Frauenplatz, opposite the fifteenth-century Church of Our Lady. According to Zehntner, Hitler and Geli spent that evening at his place of business in a private room on the first floor and did not leave until after midnight. Hitler's role in the death of Geli Raubal remained a matter of speculation.

Behind the scenes, the mole-like Bormann began to unobtrusively and systematically master all aspects of the party machinery. He became accomplished in the practice of driving wedges between his associates, then exploiting the situation to his personal benefit, and as a consequence, he was thoroughly disliked by almost everyone. With the exception of Hitler, who found him useful, nobody seemed to have a good word to say about him. His mother-in-law, Hildegard Buch, referred to him as "that swine." Hitler's architect, Albert Speer, who would later become Minister of Armaments and War Production, wrote: "Even among so many ruthless men, he stood out by his brutality and coarseness."

Whereas Göring and Göbbels reveled in notoriety and attention, Bormann preferred to operate in the wings, always away from center stage. His short, squat figure appeared in photographs with party dignitaries, but he was seldom identified by name. His face became familiar to Germans, but his name was to a large extent unknown to the general public.

His time was yet to come.

PART TWO

DOMINION AND DESCENT

In 1934, Great Britain's Parliament was troubled by protracted discussion over the lack of military preparedness. When Lord President Stanley Baldwin announced to the House of Commons that forty-one and a half squadrons were to be added to the Royal Air Force, there was an outcry from the opposition. Baldwin prophetically warned that "the old frontiers are gone. When you think of the defense of England you no longer think of the chalk cliffs of Dover; you think of the Rhine. That is where our frontier lies."

As part of the British Empire's far-flung military establishment, the Royal Warwickshire Regiment was stationed at Poona, in Southern India, where the Commander of the 1st Battalion was a little-known Lieutenant-Colonel Bernard Law Montgomery. At Goslar, a hundred miles west of Berlin in the Harz Mountains, a forty-two-year-old major named Erwin Rommel was absorbed in the minutiae of commanding the 3rd Battalion of the Reichswehr's Infantry Regiment 17. El Alamain was of no significance to either of these obscure officers.

Chapter 10

THE FIRST STEP

In German history, the First Reich (Empire) was that of Charlemagne, with the Second under Bismarck. Hitler boasted that his Third Reich would endure for a thousand years, but his confident prognostication would miss by 988 years.

After Hitler was named Chancellor on that fateful day in January 1933, General Erich Ludendorff (who had marched in the unsuccessful Beer Hall Putsch in 1923 but had since broken with Hitler) warned his old comrade-in-arms President von Hindenburg that "this sinister individual will lead our country into the abyss and our nation to an unprecedented catastrophe."

Now, in the driver's seat, the new chancellor began laying the groundwork for a course of action that would

Paul von Hindenberg

eventually fulfill that dire prophecy. With Hitler, the Nazi Party was a means to an end—an apparatus through which he could attain dictatorial power. In the strict meaning of the term, it was in actuality not a political party at all. It was, in a sense, a form of Trojan horse which Hitler manipulated to place himself in a position whereby he could grasp control of the government. He had worked within the system—as he said he would do when he was released from Landsberg Prison in 1924—and now he would methodically destroy the system to preclude others from following him up the same stairs to the top. He was a political virtuoso, deftly playing each faction against the other. By courting the labor unions, the industrialists, the bankers, the military establishment—anyone who could be of some benefit to him—he had misled them all and had climbed from the very bottom of the heap. He would now destroy them all.

When Hitler became chancellor, Germany was operating under the Weimar Constitution, so called because it was drafted by a national assembly convoked in the City of Weimar in 1919 at the end of the First World War. Under this constitution, the chancellor was somewhat like a prime minister. His main functions were to form a cabinet, influence new legislation in the Reichstag, and establish and implement government policies. However, it was the president who was the commander in chief of the armed forces with the authority to declare martial law if he deemed it necessary to restore law and order. This was the Sword of Damocles suspended over Hitler's head as he circumspectly presided over his first cabinet meeting within hours after being sworn in on January 30, 1933.

Hitler was so eager to be named chancellor that he had agreed to President von Hindenburg's plan to pack the new cabinet with non-Nazis. This was a relatively minor hindrance to the new chancellor, as under his master scheme the cabinet would eventually be rendered powerless. Other than Hitler, the only Nazis in the eleven-member cabinet were Wilhelm Frick, appointed Reich Minister of the Interior, and Hermann Göring, Minister without Portfolio and Prussian Minister of the Interior. The president's favorite (and neighbor) Franz von Papen was the new vice-chancellor. As a pretense of cooperation, Hitler carefully observed cabinet protocol at the early session, and even asked for advice. As his grip on the government tightened and he became more familiar with details and procedures, this would gradually change, and meetings became less frequent. With his bohemian background, he had some difficulty negotiating the transition to high office, especially when it came to proper attire. He was ill at ease in formal dress, and soon discarded this for the party uniform.

It did not take long for the Trojan horse to begin its odious disgorgement. Seventeen states comprised Germany, the largest being Prussia, which contained approximately two-thirds of the entire population including Berlin. Each state controlled its own police, through their separate ministries of interior. Göring found himself in charge of the Prussian police in his coveted role as Prussian Minister of the Interior, with offices at No. 3 Wilhelmstraße in Berlin. His first official act was to fire twenty-two of the thirty-two chiefs of police in his Prussian domain, replacing them with SA or SS members. He also designated the SA as an auxiliary police force. The lawbreakers now became law enforcers, responsible to Göring. In a speech he delivered in the city of Dortmund, he had these comforting words to offer:

In future there will be but one man with power and responsibility in Prussia, and that man is myself. Those who do their duty in the service of the state, obey my orders and ruthlessly use their guns when attacked can rely on my protection. Those, on the other hand, who act as cowards, have to realize that they will immediately be thrown out. A bullet fired by a policeman is a bullet that belongs to me. And if you say that is murder, then I am the murderer. I know of only two types of people: those with us and those against us.

Not content with purging the police ranks, Göring also called in Robert Kempner, a young prosecutor who was no friend of the Nazis, and insultingly fired him, shouting, "Get out of my sight, I never want to see you again!" But he did see him again. To Göring's discomfort, they would meet again in several years under drastically different circumstances. Curiously, it was after Göring assumed control of the Prussian police network that all records of his commitment to Langbro Asylum in Sweden mysteriously disappeared.[1] He now had access to the secret files of the Prussian Political Police, which contained confidential data on all politicians of all parties, which he avidly perused.

When President von Hindenburg appointed Hitler as chancellor, it was with the proviso that he obtain a working majority in the Reichstag. Accordingly, the Reichstag was again dissolved (a frequent occurrence in the dying days of the Weimar Republic), and new elections were set for March 5, 1933. Clearly, the Reichstag and everything it stood for was a source of constant vexation and

---

[1] These records were discovered later.

concern to Hitler and an impediment to his ultimate goal of totalitarianism. With control of the Prussian police now firmly in hand, and the formidable SA champing at the bit and cloaked in legality as auxiliary policemen, the next logical step was to eliminate the obstacle represented by the Reichstag. Hitler had persuaded the aged and incautious von Hindenburg to name him chancellor. Could he now inveigle the old man into granting him even more authority? The question pondered was: How could the Reichstag be circumvented and emasculated?

The answer was not long in coming.

Chapter 11

FIRE!

It happened one week before voters were scheduled to cast their ballots. At 9:14 PM on the evening of February 27, while Hitler was enjoying dinner at the Göbbelses' residence, the alarm activated at Firehouse Number 6 on Linienstraße. The impressive Reichstag building had erupted in flames and was reduced to a gutted ruin, despite the best efforts of the Berlin Fire Brigade to control the widespread conflagration. Hitler and Göbbels rushed to the site of the fire, and found a thoroughly agitated Göring already on the scene. A young Dutch Communist named Marinus van der Lubbe was spotted inside the flame-engulfed structure and promptly arrested as an arsonist. He readily acknowledged his guilt, explaining that his act of arson was "a protest," and that he was solely responsible.

The Reichstag

Göring had already decided on a plan of action as he paced the fire lines, attired in a long vicuna coat, barking orders right and left. "This," he announced theatrically, "is a crime against the new government!" The man who had twenty-eight days earlier promised the German people "honor and freedom" now declared that "every Communist deputy [of the Reichstag] must this night be strung up!" As a measure of overkill, he also asserted that "every Communist official must be shot, where he is found." He had apparently conducted an investigation, identified all conspirators, convicted them, and was ready to impose the supreme penalty—capital punishment—all within a matter of minutes after arrival at the fire.

Not to be outdone, Hitler joined in the tirade against unknown enemies of his new government. The impulsive Göring, however, was moving too fast even for Hitler, who still had to contend with von Hindenburg. Working off of arrest lists prepared in advance, the police, assisted by the newly empowered SA, began rounding up the "enemies" that very night, even before the embers of the destroyed Reichstag had cooled. The arrestees included not only Communists, but Social Democrats and pacifists. Some Reichstag deputies went into hiding to forestall arrest. Over three thousand persons were taken into custody as the Nazis crushed the phantom "revolution."

The following morning Hitler convened his cabinet and imperiously informed members that the crisis required drastic measures that could not be hampered by "legal considerations." It was an argument he would put to good use many times in the future. There was little or no opposition from within the pliant cabinet. That evening Hitler and Vice-Chancellor von Papen called on von Hindenburg. Hitler had in his possession a carefully worded emergency decree that, he explained to the wavering president, was necessary to save Germany from a Communist takeover, which had been signaled by the outrageous Reichstag fire. All that was needed was von Hindenburg's signature, which was duly affixed. The decree suspended the civil liberties of every German citizen. Abolished with a stroke of the pen were the rights of free speech, free press, and assembly. The Weimar Constitution, which had been laboriously drafted to guarantee these rights, was now thrown into the ash can, never to be retrieved. Indiscriminate house searches were now authorized without the formality of search warrants. Constitutional safeguards fell by the wayside as death penalty punishment was extended to cover a number of minor offenses.

The elections were held, as scheduled, on March 5. The Nazis received 44 percent of the votes, easily besting the opposing parties (Communists, Social Democrats, Bavarian People's Party, Nationalists, and the Center Party). However, despite the intimidation heaped upon the electorate in the final week before the election, Hitler could not capture a clear majority.

Hitler had come a long way, and he had absolutely no intention of relinquishing his hold on the chancellorship. He now carefully prepared his agenda. Göbbels had served his apprenticeship while in charge of party propaganda. Now, as a journeyman propagandist, he was appointed Minister for Propaganda and Public Enlightenment on March 14. Göbbels knew what was expected of him as he moved into his new office on Wilhemsplatz in the heart of Berlin, across from the Reich Chancellery. In a few short years he had progressed from an impecunious, unemployed, unsuccessful writer to a position in which he would control every word printed in a newspaper or magazine or uttered on radio. Hitler—through Göbbels—now exercised total mastery over the media. All periodicals, except Nazi organs, were peremptorily banned. In accordance with the "emergency decree" which von Hindenburg had been duped into signing, journalists and editors who voiced opposition were immediately jailed. On March 22 a concentration camp was opened at Dachau, and was soon filled with dissenters of all political hues. To justify incarceration, all that was necessary was a charge of "suspicion of activities inimical to the state." The lights of freedom were beginning to flicker throughout Germany.

Göbbels even used his new authority to coerce his wife's former husband into surrendering custody of his ten-year-old son, Harold. Gunther Quandt, who had viewed the Nazi movement with disdain, was called into Göbbels's office, and in a high-handed manner advised that the youngster would henceforth be living in the Göbbels household because of the father's "negative influence." When the respected industrialist objected and pointed out that the courts had awarded him custody in the divorce decree, Göbbels insolently called him a "swine" and threatened him with ruination. Quandt had little choice but to yield. Nevertheless, on May 3 he was arrested and held in custody for three months. He was never given a reason for his arrest, and no charge was ever brought against him. It was an example of the frightening power Hitler had given Göbbels.

The chancellor was now ready with his coup de grace. The new Reichstag, with the Nazis holding 288 seats, convened the day before Dachau opened. With the Reichstag building destroyed, the session was held in Berlin's Kroll Opera House. Two days later, on March 23, Hitler delivered a speech to the deputies that was reminiscent of his campaign rhetoric—something for everybody. But there was a catch. What he needed to effectively govern, he intoned, was a special statute which he called "The Law for Alleviating the Distress of People and Reich." The term was a classic misnomer. This "enabling act" would transfer legislative power from the Reichstag to Hitler's cabinet, but inasmuch as it meant a constitutional change, a two-thirds vote of the Reichstag was required. Thanks to the "emergency decree" injudiciously signed into law on February 28, Communist deputies were either in jail or in hiding. With the opposition reduced to a minimum, and with SA and SS men in ominous evidence everywhere, the matter was put to a vote. The measure was enacted into law by a margin of 441 to 84. Hitler had successfully played his trump card. The death knell had been sounded for parliamentary government in Germany. The impressive opera house was a fitting setting for the requiem. The date was March 23, 1933. Hitler had been in office less than two months. When he asked the deputies of the Reichstag to approve the "enabling act," he made a pledge he had no intention of honoring: "The government will make use of these powers only insofar as they are essential for carrying out vitally necessary measures. . . . The number of cases in which an internal necessity exists for having recourse to such a law is in itself a limited one." In actuality, the Reichstag ceased to exist. There was never another free election in Germany during the lifetime of Adolf Hitler.

On July 13 William E. Dodd and his family arrived in Berlin by train from Hamburg, where they had disembarked from the liner SS *Washington*. Dodd was President Franklin D. Roosevelt's appointee as the new American ambassador to Germany. As Dodd's twenty-four-year-old daughter Martha traveled to her hotel from the Lehrter train station, she passed the gutted Reichstag building.

Martha asked what had happened. Her escort, an embassy secretary, uneasily replied: "Young lady, you must learn to be seen and not heard. You mustn't say so much and ask so many questions. This isn't America and you can't say all the things you think." Such was Martha Dodd's introduction to Nazi Germany.

To this day controversy surrounds the burning of the Reichstag. Lubbe, the avowed arsonist, was convicted and quickly beheaded, after a trial during which he appeared

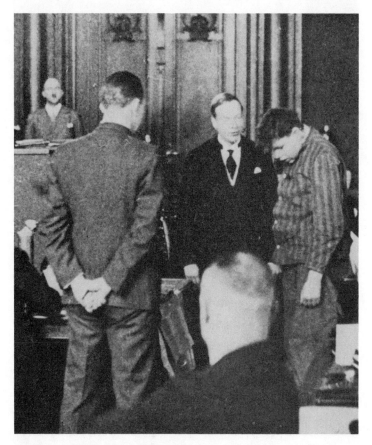

The trial of Marinus van der Lubbe

Franz Halder claimed to have heard Hermann Göring admit
responsibility for the Reichstag fire.

to be drugged. Although there was no evidence linking them to the case, four other persons were also arrested and charged with the crime. They were all Communists and one, Ernst Torgler, a Reichstag deputy. Fortunately for them, in 1933 the courts in Germany still exercised a degree of independence (although this was rapidly eroding) and the quartet was exonerated. Torgler, however, was then placed in "protective custody" despite his acquittal.

The consensus was (and still is) that the Nazis themselves were responsible for the arson, and that Lubbe was merely a dupe. An underground heating system passage connected the Reichstag to the palace of the Reichstag president, which in turn was occupied by Göring. The thesis is that Göbbels, with the connivance of Göring, masterminded the plot and helped select the arson squad headed by SA leader Karl Ernst, also a Reichstag deputy. It was significant that Hitler and all of the top Nazis were in Berlin the evening of February 27 and within a close proximity to the Reichstag building, despite the fact that this was a scant week before a national election in which they were all feverishly involved. It was notable that Göring had arrest lists already prepared when he arrived at the scene of the fire, and that by the next day Hitler had a cleverly drafted "emergency decree" ready for von Hindenburg's signature. The entire scenario had the earmarks of a scheme that proceeded to fruition precisely as planned, and appeared to be part of Hitler's overall agenda to seize control of all governmental processes.

A 1964 book by German Fritz Tobias submitted that Lubbe was the only person responsible for the fire, and that the Nazis were entirely blameless. Although a few chroniclers (including the American writer John Toland) were swayed, the majority of historians have not changed their original opinion. Heinrich Fränkel, who has coauthored several well-researched books on the Nazis, conducted his own inquiry and interviewed a woman who told him that a few days before the fire, she dealt with Lubbe in her capacity as a district nurse in Berlin, at which time the young vagrant was in the company of two members of the SA. This is in direct contradiction to Tobias's assertion that Lubbe did not have any contact with the SA prior to the fire. It has also been established that Karl Ernst was a frequent visitor to Göring's office prior to February 27.

Moreover, Nazi experts Konrad Heiden and Willi Frischauer were working as newspapermen in Germany in 1933, and both have written extensively on the Nazi participation in the plot. Frischauer was the Berlin correspondent for the Vienna newspaper, *Wiener Allgemeine Zeitung,* and on the night of the fire cabled a story to his editors that included these words: "There can scarcely be any doubt that the fire which is now destroying the Reichstag was set by henchmen of the Hitler government. By all appearances, the arsonists used an underground passage connecting the Reichstag to the palace of its president, Hermann Göring."

Karl Dietrich Bracher, professor of political science and contemporary history at the University of Bonn, refers to the Tobias work as "revisionist reinterpretation," and terms it "questionable." Hans Bernd Gisevius, who served in the Gestapo and the Prussian Ministry of Interior (and who was certainly in a position to know) testified at Nuremberg that the Nazis staged the entire incident. Also at the Nuremberg trials, General Franz Halder, former Chief of the Army General Staff, offered this incriminating piece of evidence:

Kurt Dalüge

> At a luncheon on the birthday of the Führer in 1942 the conversation turned to the topic of the Reichstag building and its artistic value. I heard with my own ears when Göring interrupted the conversation and shouted: "The only one who really knows about the Reichstag is I, because I set it on fire."

Not unexpectedly, there was a denial from defendant Göring.

An international committee convened in Luxembourg in 1969 to consider all aspects of the fire. The Swiss historian Walther Hofer chaired the committee, which concluded that indeed the Nazis were the culpable parties. The committee's findings rearranged the cast, and rejected the "lone arsonist" theory. The final reports suggested that Heydrich's fine hand was involved in the planning and execution of the plot, and that a team of arsonists led by SA Standartenführer Erwin Villain went to Göring's palace at least forty-eight hours before the planned fire, and even took cots with them to sleep on.

The committee's findings have been endorsed by a number of knowledgeable historians, both German and American. The list includes Dr. Karl Dietrich Erdmann, Klaus Hildebrandt, and Dr. Otto B. Rögele, director of the Institute of Journalistic Science of the University of Münich. The American author Gordon A. Craig covered this subject in his book, *Germany 1866–1945*, and wrote:

> Despite recent attempts, however, to support the case against Marinus van der Lubbe, the half-witted Dutch vagrant who was tried and executed for the crime, the evidence collected by the international committee headed by Walther Hofer of Berne strongly supports the conclusion that the blaze was set by SA/SS Sondergruppe

under the direction of Himmler's associate, Reinhard Heydrich, and the director of the division of police in the Prussian Ministry of the Interior, Kurt Dalüge.

On the basis of informed judgment and in the face of what occurred before, during, and immediately after the Reichstag fire, to maintain that the Nazis were uninvolved is to strain the credulity of the objective researcher.

Rudolf Diels. As first head of the Gestapo, he found time to romance the American ambassador's daughter.

Chapter 12

THE HIT LIST

With the signing of the emergency decree and the passage of the enabling act, Hitler had in just two months—quite legally—become dictator of Germany.

On May 2, 1933, he struck at the working class by ordering the SA and the SS to seize trade union offices throughout the Reich. Union officials were arrested and union bank accounts confiscated. Hitler began to methodically extend his influence into every sphere of German life. His clutch was to be ever-tightening. Göring insured that the grasp would never relax when in April 1933 he created a new police agency, to be named *Geheime Staatspolizei* (Secret State Police, or "Gestapo" for short). It was a name that became synonymous with Nazi tyranny.

The Gestapo was not a law enforcement agency in the usual meaning of the term, as it did not concern itself with crime prevention or investigation into such criminal offenses as murder, robbery, burglary, or rape. Instead it was a political force whose only real function was to protect the interests of the state (which meant Hitler and his adherents). It operated with impunity, and in due time had jurisdiction over every square foot of land controlled by Hitler, epitomizing the meaning of "police state." Göring, who was given a virtual blank check by Hitler in running the new force, appointed Rudolf Diels (formerly with the Prussian Political Police) as the first Chief of the Gestapo. The all-powerful agency established headquarters at No. 8 Prinz Albrechtstraße in Berlin, and Diels was given authority to draw his agents from the ranks of the SA and the SS.

Göring had inherited Diels, a thirty-four-year-old lawyer, when he assumed administrative control of the Prussian Political Police. Diels had been a Social Democrat, and was one of the few "outsiders" or former non-Nazis to gain a foothold in the upper echelons of Hitler's police structure. The crafty Diels was regarded by many of his colleagues as an opportunist—and with good reason.

Just as Hitler needed Göring, Göring needed Diels—at least at the onset. As chief of the Prussian Political Police, Diels had amassed a wealth of information on politicians of all parties, and Göring could ill afford not to avail himself of Diels's expertise and knowledge. Tall and slim, the graduate of the University of Marburg had a disarming smile that belied his cunning. His face was laced with several dueling scars. He had a way with women and had acquired a reputation for sexual prowess. He was often seen at social affairs, attending numerous afternoon teas and diplomatic dinners or luncheons, always charming, ever gracious with the ladies. It was in one of these social settings that he met Martha Dodd, the American ambassador's strong-willed daughter. She soon succumbed to his attentions, and it was not long before she started a somewhat brazen relationship with him. They frequented various nightclubs, dancing, enjoying themselves. The suave Gestapo chief, estranged from his wife, knew his way around Berlin. He was as comfortable in the social whirl as he was in the realm of political intrigue or harsh police activity.

To gain advantage over potential rivals both within and outside of the party, Göring also established a Directorate of Scientific Research, which was a misleading title for a unit whose primary purpose was to tap telephones and transcribe the conversations for his own edification. This extensive monitoring program invaded the privacy of just about everybody who amounted to anything (except Hitler). Göring was disconcerted to learn that Röhm and Karl Ernst referred to his girlfriend, Emmy Sonnemann, as "Göring's sow."

While Göring was taking steps to abrogate the rights of the citizenry, Göbbels was busy in his own realm. The frustrated writer who could never sell a single manuscript had decided that he would be the judge of what constituted suitable reading for the public. As an encore to the burning of the Reichstag, an event occurred that was reminiscent of a Middle Ages ritual—the burning of books that Göbbels determined were detrimental to German culture. That is, his interpretation of German culture. On May 10 unruly gangs of Nazi zealots looted public and private libraries of proscriptive books in several cities, then consigned the books to ceremonious bonfires. The Propaganda Minister hailed the action of the frenzied book burners on a national radio broadcast as the flames consumed the works of such diverse authors as Jack London, Sigmund Freud, Thomas Mann, Erich Maria Remarque, Albert Einstein, Upton Sinclair, Helen Keller, Margaret Sanger, Émile Zola, Havelock Ellis, and H. G. Wells.

The other members of Hitler's inner clique were beginning to flex their muscles and move into control positions in the new government. On April 21 Rudolf Hess was appointed to the newly created post of Deputy to the Führer. On December 1, 1933, he became a member of Hitler's cabinet, and one of his duties was to maintain cooperation between the SA and the Nazi Party. He became, in effect, the chancellor's administrative assistant. He was even given authority to modify sentences imposed by the courts, with the aim of increasing penalties if deemed appropriate. In July 1933 Hess acquired a Chief of Staff— Martin Bormann. At the time, little significance was given to that promotion. Since it was no longer necessary for new legislation to be routed through the impotent Reichstag, it was Hess and/or Bormann who drafted and signed most of Hitler's decrees—all of which became absolute law in Germany, without recourse to legal review or redress.

As the first Christmas under Nazi rule neared, Göring was becoming uneasy as Röhm began to assume the role of strongman. While deliberately limiting the size of the SS, Röhm continued to expand the SA by leaps and bounds until his private strike force reached an incredible number of almost three million, larger than the combined complements of the army, navy, and air force.

Now that Göring had "learned the ropes," he regarded Diels as expendable; he also questioned the trustworthiness of the ex-Social Democrat. The insecure chief of the Gestapo had the feeling he had outlived his usefulness, especially when he discovered that his own telephone was being tapped by his boss. On one occasion Göring confronted Diels with the accusation he was being cozy with Röhm, and said to him: "I warn you, Diels, you can't sit on both sides of the fence." Diels answered: "Herr Minister President, the Head of the Secret State Police must sit on all sides of the fence at once." It was not the response Göring wanted, and Diels (who had many enemies) realized his days were numbered. According to what he later divulged, at a meeting with Göring and Hitler at Berchtesgaden, he was told to draw up a plan by which Röhm, von Schleicher, and other prominent persons would be slain. For whatever reason, he demurred. Afterwards, he requested a leave of absence, pleading illness.

Diels's tenure with the Gestapo was about to end. He was ousted from his job, and Göring angrily rebuked him: "You have disappointed, compromised, and abandoned me. Look to your own future." The ax officially fell on April 20 when hard-liner Nazi ideologist Himmler was named as the new Gestapo Chief. Diels was fortunate in that he was shunted to the sidelines with an appointment as Regional Commissioner of Cologne. Himmler was now in command of both the SS and the Gestapo, with Heydrich his second-in-command.

Himmler's fortunes were improving dramatically. He no longer suffered the undignified association with the chicken farm (he had sold the Waldtrudering property), having moved his place of residence to a little town named Gmund in the picturesque Tegernsee area. Upon appointment as Gestapo head, he himself moved into a villa in a prosperous suburb of Berlin, leaving his wife and daughter at Gmund, where he visited them infrequently. He took over at Gestapo headquarters in Berlin at the Prinz Albrechtstraße, while Heydrich's offices were established nearby in the Wilhelmstraße.

Röhm also bettered his living quarters, as well as his standard of living. He occupied a richly appointed mansion in Berlin's Tiergartenstraße, which became the scene of bacchanalian revelry with his homosexual friends. Although Hitler had given Röhm a free hand to supervise and enlarge the SA—and this was doubtless the arrangement when Röhm agreed to return from Bolivia—it was obvious the chancellor and the chief of staff of the SA had different goals in sight. Hitler had scarcely settled into his new offices in the Chancellery when Röhm demanded his share of the victory spoils. For one thing, he wanted the SA put on the same level as the Reichswehr, or—more precisely—the Reichswehr absorbed into the SA, a prospect that appalled the professional officer corps. More than anything else, he wanted to be Minister of Defense, in charge of all the armed forces. This is not what Der Führer had in mind.

On December 1, 1933, Röhm was brought into the cabinet, and a month later Hitler sent him a glowing letter which ended with the cordial paragraph:

> At the close of the year of the National Socialist Revolution, therefore, I feel compelled to thank you, my dear Ernst Röhm, for the imperishable services you have rendered to the National Socialist movement and the German people, and to assure you how very grateful I am to Fate that I am able to call such men as you my friends and fellow combatants.
>
> In true friendship and grateful regard,
> *Your Adolf Hitler*

Röhm, however, was not to be satisfied with these crumbs. He had known Hitler when the chancellor was a nobody, and he was not appeased with what he interpreted as empty gestures designed to relegate him to limbo. While this mollification tactic may have worked on others, it was wasted on the headstrong ex-Reichswehr captain. On June 4, 1934, he and Hitler engaged in a rancorous showdown at the Chancellery in an unsuccessful attempt to resolve their differences. Whatever Röhm's faults, a lackey he was not. But what he did not know was that two months earlier, on April 11, in a secret meeting aboard the cruiser *Deutschland*, Hitler had struck a deal with the military: In return for the support of the navy and the regular army, he would handle Röhm and the SA.

Since becoming chancellor, Hitler had been able to exercise personal control over all of his top-level appointees—except Röhm. Röhm presented a special problem because he was backed by the SA, and the Brownshirts supported their leader. From the earliest days of their long association, Hitler had been aware of Röhm's sexual propensities, which he conveniently overlooked. Now that he had attained his goal and no longer needed him, he professed to be outraged by the SA chief's personal conduct.

As the summer of 1934 approached, and Röhm continued to rock the boat, Hitler had a decision to make. Although his tentacles encircled the German people and he had the tools of suppression at his disposal, he could not countenance the fact that opposition to his authority still existed. For years he had criticized the state. It was a privilege he would now ruthlessly deny others. He well knew that people like von Schleicher and Gregor Strasser would welcome an alliance with an unconstrained Röhm if it would mean the downfall of Adolf Hitler. Under no circumstances could he allow the incubation of this dangerous amalgam, however unlikely it might be. His enemies did not realize that Hitler was not just another politician.

Tension was heightened on June 17, 1934, when Vice-Chancellor von Papen, in an astonishing display of bravado, delivered an eloquent address at the University of Marburg, sharply criticizing the government's oppressive policies and calling for the restoration of freedom of the press. "It is time," von Papen told his audience, "to come together in brotherly love and respect for our fellow countrymen." This had never been Hitler's policy, was not now his policy, and never would be. This message to the students and faculty by von Papen was the last public speech of dissent ever delivered in Nazi Germany. Copies of the speech were distributed, despite frantic efforts by Göbbels to prevent dissemination. Von Papen still had the president's ear, and Hitler fully realized that if von Hindenburg was persuaded to declare martial law, everything he had worked for over the years would be snatched away. Hitler had no intention of permitting any further expression of dissidence.

Der Führer could wait no longer. When he had decided to neutralize the Reichstag and remove the impediment represented by the constitution, he had merely faked the menace of a Communist revolution with an act of arson. Now that he was faced with a threat to his leadership, he reverted to the formula that had proved so successful in the spring of 1933. His solution was quite simple: Invent a plot to overthrow the government, and then kill those he claimed were involved in the conspiracy.

With utmost secrecy a death list was compiled. Heydrich was in control of the master list, which was expanded almost daily as they added more names of "enemies of the party." Working out of Gestapo headquarters, Heydrich meticulously correlated the planning for the operation which was assigned the disarming and innocuous code name of KOLIBRI (hummingbird). As the target date neared, sealed envelopes containing instructions were distributed to various Gestapo units throughout Germany.

███ ██ ▒▒▒▒ ───

Bella Fromm had become one of the most informed and well-known journalists in Berlin. She wrote an American-style society column for two dailies, *Vossische Zeitung* and *Berliner Zeitung*, both published by the influential House of Ullstein, a major media firm. In actuality, however, she was much more than a society writer. Over the years, she had developed an eclectic network of contacts in Berlin's social, political, and diplomatic circles, and she made it a practice to keep her ear to the ground. The so-called Editors' Law of October 1933—which excluded non-Aryans from the field of journalism—forced her employers to dismiss her because of her Jewishness, but she still maintained her many sources of information. As the month of June 1934 drew to a close, she perceived that a portentous uneasiness prevailed. Something was about to happen, but she couldn't quite put her finger on it.

Bella counted among her trusted friends former chancellor von Schleicher and his new bride, Elizabeth. On June 22 she invited them to her residence for dinner, along with another old friend, General Ferdinand von Bredow, who had been a former assistant to von Schleicher in the Defense Ministry. She tried to convey her apprehension to von Schleicher, and warned him to be careful, but he dismissed her concern, saying, "They won't dare to touch me." She wasn't convinced. Von Schleicher made an attempt to reassure her: "The same old Bella. Alarmist as usual. Good Lord, I've been out of politics and am happy to be out of the dirty mess. So why should I

Alfried Krupp

fear?" In little more than one week Bella Fromm's dinner guests would learn the true meaning of Hitlerism.

On June 26 Rudolf Hess, Hitler's dependable deputy and emissary, visited Heydrich's office, where the two men remained behind locked doors for an extended period. When Hess departed, Heydrich reappeared in the ante-room with another list which was duly integrated.

Events now moved quickly. Two days later Hitler was in Essen where he attended a wedding of a local gauleiter, Josef Terboven. On that same day Röhm was expelled from the German Officers' League. It was a date that also marked the fifteenth anniversary of the Treaty of Versailles, and flags flew at half-mast on government buildings to remind Germans of the ignominious occasion. While Hitler was in the Ruhr, he took the opportunity to call on the Krupp family, the wealthy and famous armaments manufacturers. It was all part of an elaborate stratagem to allay any suspicions that may have been aroused when the Reichswehr (pursuant to the "Pact of the Deutschland") was placed on a state of alert and all leaves cancelled.

From Essen Hitler telephoned Röhm, who was enjoying a holiday at the Hanselbauer Hotel at Bad Wiessee on the shores of the Tegernsee, forty miles south of München. He advised the unsuspecting Röhm that he would be at Bad Wiessee at 11 AM on June 30 for an important conference, and that all high-ranking SA officers should be called to attend the meeting. Röhm immediately dispatched telegrams to the principal SA officers, ordering them to report to Bad Wiessee in accordance with Hitler's request. The obliging Röhm scheduled a banquet, with a specially ordered vegetarian menu for Hitler.

Departing Essen, Hitler proceeded to Godesberg on the Rhine where he was joined by Göbbels at the Hotel

Dreesen. While Hitler was spending an anxious Friday evening at the Hotel conferring with his aides and receiving and initiating telephone calls, the unconcerned Röhm relaxed at the Hotel Hanselbauer. He was under treatment for a form of neuralgia, and had been receiving a series of injections administered by his personal physician, Dr. Emil Ketterer, head of the SA Medical Services. Oblivious to the impending peril, Röhm joined Dr. Ketterer and a Gruppenführer Bergmann in playing Tarok, a three-handed Bavarian card game. When the card-playing session broke up at 11 PM, Röhm retired to his room for the night after being given the final injection by Dr. Ketterer.

In the meantime, Göring (who had accompanied Hitler to Terboven's wedding in Essen) returned to Berlin to finalize the assassination plans in that sector. His cousin, Herbert Göring, had at one time offered the revealing observation that Hermann would "trample over corpses" to get what he wanted. He would now prepare to do just that.

The stage was set.

Chapter 13

FLIGHT OF THE HUMMINGBIRD

A deadly game was about to be played out in Germany. It commenced early in the morning of Saturday, June 30. After a twenty-minute drive from Godesberg to Hangelar airfield in a large black Mercedes, Hitler and his entourage left Bonn by air at 2 AM. Hans Baur, Hitler's personal pilot, was at the controls.

As was his custom, Hitler sat next to the pilot—his favorite seat while flying—and as the trimotor Junker sped through the darkened skies, the former Lufthansa chief pilot would call out the name of each town or locality as they passed over. Hitler sat hunched forward, staring ahead, saying nothing, his thoughts obviously elsewhere. The plane landed about 4 AM at Oberweißenfeld Airdrome near Münich, where helmeted soldiers had been waiting for an hour. The group headed directly to the Ministry of Interior where the Münich Chief of Police, August Schneidhuber, who was also the highest-ranking SA leader of Münich, had already been placed under arrest. Schneidhuber was brought before Hitler, who flew into a hysterical rage. The agitated Führer rushed at the startled official, tore off his epaulets, and cursed him as a traitor.

"Keep your dirty fingers off of my person!" Schneidhuber yelled, unable to fathom the reason for Hitler's outburst.

"Lock him up!" the fuming Hitler retorted.

The puzzled SA leader was dragged out of the room and transported to a cell in Münich's Stadelheim Prison.

Shortly after dawn, Hitler headed for Bad Wiessee where Röhm and other SA leaders were still asleep in the Hanselbauer Hotel. This hotel, now known as the Hotel Lederer, still stands today at the edge of the quiet waters of the Tegernsee. It was not quite 7 AM when Hitler and his two-car raiding party, which included Göbbels, rolled up to the hotel entrance. They stealthily entered the hotel, and after Hitler had strategically positioned his men, a plainclothes officer knocked on the door of Röhm's room. It was a rude awakening for the SA chief of staff. "What— you here already?" he asked sleepily. He had expected Hitler—but not at this hour and certainly not in this manner. With revolver in hand, Hitler informed his compatriot and old political ally that he was under arrest.

Also awakened and arrested were several other SA officers in other rooms, including the homosexual Edmund Heines, SA leader of Breslau, who was found in bed with his chauffeur. Along with Röhm, they were placed in commandeered vehicles, and the procession headed back toward Münich. The caravan passed hundreds of citizens

Hotel Lederer, Bad Wiessee, Germany (formerly Hotel Hanselbauer), where Operation Kolibri was launched on June 30, 1934

along the road, engrossed in the routine of their daily lives, unaware that the Chancellor of Germany had just driven by with a carload of prisoners—many marked for death.

At the Münich railroad station, the SA leaders were beginning to arrive, pursuant to Röhm's telegrams. As they alighted from the incoming trains they were taken into custody by SS troops and whisked to Stadelheim Prison.

Hitler now proceeded to the Brown House, the SA headquarters on the Briennerstraße, which was to be his command post for the remainder of the day.

With the initial and critical phase of the operation successfully completed, Hitler gave the order everyone had been awaiting. At 10 AM the signal for the massacres was given. Göbbels picked up the telephone and contacted Göring in Berlin, uttering the prearranged code name: KOLIBRI.

The Rubicon had been passed. There was no turning back now.

The room occupied by Ernst Röhm when he was personally arrested by Adolf Hitler on June 30, 1934, as it looks today at the Hotel Lederer.

When the impatient Heydrich received the green light in Berlin, he moved speedily. Orders were instantly relayed to teams of killers poised throughout the Reich, utilizing telephones and the Gestapo teleprinter network. Sealed envelopes were torn open, lists scanned, and the hunt was on. The victims were relentlessly pursued by teams of Gestapo and SS men, working mostly in twos and threes.

In Münich, Berlin, Stettin, Breslau, Dresden, Gleiwitz, and other cities, the purge was implemented with brutal efficiency. Hitler sat by the telephones in Münich, assisted by Hess, and checked names off the death list as he received reports. Sepp Dietrich, commander of Hitler's SS Bodyguard, was to direct the executions at Münich's Stadelheim Prison, where all of the SA officers arrested at the Münich railroad station, as well as those bagged at Bad Wiessee with Röhm, were confined. Behind closed doors in the meeting room of the Brown House, Hitler huddled with Hess, Göbbels, Bormann, and others as the fate of the Stadelheim prisoners was decided. Finally, Bormann opened the door and beckoned to the waiting Dietrich, who entered the inner sanctum. Bormann thrust a list of names at Dietrich, while Hitler gave him verbal orders to proceed to Stadelheim and summarily execute everyone on the list.

Alfred Leitgen, adjutant to Hess, was present as Dietrich went over the list, reading aloud the names, and he later recalled what happened when Dietrich uttered the name of Hess's friend Schneidhuber:

> My boss was deathly pale, but outwardly quite calm when Dietrich began reading the names. But when the name Schneidhuber was read, Hess made a startled gesture, threw his head back and mumbled something. He

Sepp Dietrich always maintained that he was only following orders.

then bent down to whisper a few words to Hitler. Hitler shook his head with displeasure.

The name of August Schneidhuber remained on the list, despite Hess's effort to intercede.

When Dietrich arrived at the prison, he was met by Hans Frank, the Bavarian Minister of Justice, who protested that the executions could not be carried out unless there was formal, written authorization. At Frank's insistence, Dietrich telephoned the Brown House and talked to Hess, then handed the instrument to Frank with the remark that Hitler wanted to talk directly to the minister. When Frank started to object to the inadequacy of the execution orders, he was berated by the chancellor for interfering with his authority. All that was necessary, he advised Frank, was his decision to kill these people. Frank's resistance quickly wilted. His concern about legal proprieties was a short-lived aberration. He was later to become Hitler's choice as governor-general of occupied Poland, and in that role Frank relished his assigned job of killing off the Polish intelligentsia.

Dietrich now walked through the corridors of the prison facility, shouting at the occupants of the various cells: "The Führer has condemned you to death for high treason. Heil Hitler!" When he stopped in front of Cell No. 504, Schneidhuber sprang to his feet and pressed against the bars.

"Comrade Sepp!" he cried. "This is madness. We are innocent."

But Dietrich had already moved on to the next cell, repeating the same terrifying words. And then on to the next cell. Schneidhuber's entreaties fell on deaf ears, and he was taken to the courtyard where six SS riflemen waited for their human targets. From Cell No. 474, Röhm could hear the familiar sound of rifle fire. His fate was to be delayed. A decade later, as Commander of the Sixth Panzer Army, Dietrich would be responsible for the murder of captured American prisoners of war during the Battle of the Bulge.

In Berlin, everything was progressing on schedule under the direction of Göring and Himmler. Moving rapidly and by strict design, SS men and Göring's special police surrounded the SA headquarters and seized it without resistance. Within minutes Göring arrived on the scene, and ran through the building, pointing at individuals and shouting, "Arrest him! Arrest him! Arrest him!" Every person so designated was doomed.

Some 150 SA leaders were thus arrested either at headquarters or at their homes and taken to the Cadet School at Lichterfelde Barracks, twenty miles southeast of Berlin, and locked in a cellar. They were then methodically slaughtered in the most callous manner imaginable.

There was no judicial process. At brief intervals, four names were called out, and the luckless quartet removed from the cellar and marched to the red brick wall of the courtyard where their shirts were ripped off and a circle drawn around their left nipple with charcoal.

From a window in the cellar the prisoners whose names had not yet been called watched in grotesque fascination as eight SS sharpshooters blasted away from a distance of five or six yards, the bullets tearing out hunks of flesh as they penetrated the prisoners' torsos. The gory pieces stuck to the wall where the darker segments from the heart were distinguishable. No effort was made to clean the wall between executions, and before long the brick wall was completely covered with blood and fragments of flesh. After a period of time, even the eight men of the firing squad became unnerved at the hideous carnage, and had to be replaced with a fresh crew of riflemen.

Germany's largest city was a study in incongruity on this last day of June. While murderous teams of Gestapo agents and SS men scoured the community seeking their quarry, unwitting Berliners went about this business as usual. Outwardly it was just another hot, clear summer Saturday, with a temperature forecast of 86 degrees. Nazi flags rippled in a slight breeze above government buildings. Couples strolled along Unter den Linden, and patrons sipped coffee in the many terrace cafes.

At No. 8 Prinz Albrechtstraße, Heydrich received a constant stream of reports from his agents, which he then forwarded to Göring who had set up a clearinghouse in his study at the prime minister's palace in the Leipzigerstraße. During the course of the day, shouts of excitement and raucous laughter could be heard from within the room as Göring and his staff—between sandwiches and bottles of beer—reviewed progress reports on the dragnet.

Amidst this savageness, the sadistic Göring indulged in a macabre joke at the expense of Gehrt, his old comrade in arms, who had served with him in the Richthofen Squadron and like Göring had been awarded the Pour le Merite. Gehrt, now an SA leader, was summoned from the cellar at Lichterfelde Barracks, and expected to be led to the wall. Instead, he was given unexplained instructions.

"Go home," he was told, "and put on your uniform with your medals, and report to Prime Minister Göring."

Gehrt hastily followed orders—thinking he had been reprieved—and was ushered into Göring's presence where the man who would become commander in chief of the Luftwaffe was surrounded by his staff. Any thought that his friendship with Göring might save his life was soon dispelled.

"You filthy pig!" Göring shouted at the stunned Gehrt, tearing off his Pour le Merite. "I wanted to deal with you myself! Take him away!"

Returned to the cellar, Gehrt was completely shattered by the harrowing experience before Göring. Within an hour his name was called again, and it was necessary to push him to the wall.

Some of the victims at Lichterfelde Barracks didn't even know why they were being killed. Some thought the operation to be anti-Hitler, and many died at the wall professing their loyalty to the chancellor and shouting "Heil Hitler!" as the triggers were pulled.

Karl Ernst was on his honeymoon, but was intercepted near Bremen en route to Madeira. He was Röhm's chief of the Berlin SA, and the suspected leader of the Reichstag arson team. He did not take his arrest seriously. After all, hadn't Hitler been his witness at his recent wedding? He was incredulous as he was handcuffed.

"Everything will be straightened out when we get to Berlin," he assured his captors.

Ernst was flown back to Berlin where a check mark was duly entered opposite his name on the annihilation list. He joined the procession to the wall at Lichterfelde Barracks, where the bodies of the slain were loaded on a horse-drawn meat truck that was driven to a small village nearby named Schmargendorf where the remains were cremated. After each trip the empty conveyance returned for another pile of corpses.

The purge was by no means limited to the SA leadership. Many citizens were individually hunted down and murdered that weekend because they knew too much, or for no other reason that at one time or another they had opposed the Nazi hierarchy. Personal vengeance snuffed out more than one life.

Three men had helped von Papen formulate the speech he made on June 17 at the University of Marburg: Dr. Erich Klausener, Edgar Jung, and Herbert von Bose. Dr. Klausener was a prominent Berliner and respected Catholic layman. He was a director in the Ministry of Transport, president of Catholic Action in Berlin, member of the Order of St. Gregory, as well as a Knight of the Iron Cross, First Class. Two SS men entered his office and advised him that he was under arrest. Klausener arose and started to follow them, but was shot dead before he had taken two steps. As he had been instructed by Heydrich, triggerman Kurt Gildisch then placed the gun in the dead man's hand in an attempt to disguise the murder as a suicide.

Jung's housekeeper found his apartment ransacked. On a wall in the bathroom she saw the word *Gestapo* penciled in his handwriting. It was self-explanatory. When notified of his friend's disappearance, von Papen protested to Himmler.

"A simple inquiry," the Gestapo chief explained.

Jung—a journalist and an attorney—was never seen alive again.

Von Bose was shot at his desk at the Vice-Chancellery. A person in an adjoining office heard eleven shots.

Von Papen escaped execution mainly because he was a personal friend of President von Hindenburg, who was still a national hero despite his advanced age. The vice-chancellor was placed under house arrest and became a prisoner in his own home, with his telephone lines severed. When he learned of this development, American Ambassador Dodd was concerned. He drove slowly past the residence, and then stopped to leave his card at the door. Von Papen survived and inside of a month was given an assignment as Hitler's minister to Vienna. He subsequently played a key part in the Third Reich's diplomatic machinations.

Two Gestapo agents proceeded to Otto Strasser's home in Oranienburg and quietly let themselves in through the locked door with a skeleton key. Their intended victim, however, had seen the handwriting on the wall and had—with the aid of a false passport—fled to Vienna where he was living under the assumed name of Franz Baumann. His brother Gregor was not so fortunate.

Spurning Otto's counsel to join him in exile, Gregor chose to remain in the Fatherland. It was a grievous decision, as Hitler still considered him a potential rival. Gregor was having lunch with his family in Berlin on June 30 when he was abruptly arrested by five SS men and taken to Prinz Albrechtstraße Gestapo jail. When he saw the barrel of a pistol pointed toward him through the bars, he tried to hide—but he was beyond succor. He was caught in a fusillade of bullets, one of which ruptured an artery. The cell suddenly resembled an abattoir as the mortally wounded Gregor lurched and slipped about in his own blood. As Strasser's life ebbed away, Reinhard Heydrich peered into the small cell and asked: "Isn't he dead yet? Let the swine bleed to death."

Former chancellor von Schleicher, who had tried to circumvent Hitler by offering the vice-chancellorship to Gregor Strasser, was sitting in the study of his villa at Neubabelsberg near Potsdam, going over household accounts with his housekeeper, Marie Guntel, while his wife sat in a nearby armchair doing some knitting. In response to the incessant ringing of the garden doorbell, the housekeeper opened the door to be confronted by five SS men in plainclothes. The assassins pushed past her, holding drawn revolvers behind their backs. Following Frau

Franz von Papen

Kurt von Schleicher

Guntel into the study, one of the men asked: "Are you General von Schleicher?" When the General answered "yes," the gunmen started shooting, as the terrified house-keeper ran screaming into the garden. When the SS men drove off one minute later, von Schleicher and his bride of eighteen months lay dead. Bella Fromm's foreboding had become reality.

The gunfire at the von Schleicher villa was heard at the Adenauer residence a few hundred yards away. Konrad Adenauer was in the garden with his family, watering his flowers, when a Gestapo agent climbed over the locked garden gate and arrested him. He was permitted to pack a few belongings, and then driven away. Later, interrogated at the Potsdam police headquarters, he was threatened with torture but adamantly denied complicity in any type of anti-Nazi activity. He was released unharmed after two days, but after receiving a confidential message that he was still in danger, he left home and disappeared for several weeks, moving from place to place. It was a strange and un-chronicled interlude in his life, as he did not communicate with his family during his absence. The fifty-eight-year-old Adenauer had already been mayor of Cologne and president of the Prussian State Council, but his most impressive achievements were yet to come. The man who in 1934 was considered "nationally unreliable" by the Nazis became the chancellor of postwar Germany, leading his country to economic recovery and respectability out of the rubble left by Hitler.

A few hours after the murder of von Schleicher and his wife, General von Bredow (who eight days earlier had enjoyed dinner with the von Schleichers on Bella Fromm's garden terrace) sat at a table at the Hotel Adlon in the heart of Berlin. When he left, the waiter—a Gestapo informant—picked up his tip, and then made a telephone call. When von Bredow reached his home he was gunned down on his doorstep.

Seventy-three-year-old Gustav von Kahr was found in a swamp near Dachau, mutilated and hacked to death. He had been the key prosecution witness against Hitler in the 1924 treason trial, and the new chancellor had a long memory. Now that Hitler had autocratic control, there would be no trial for von Kahr, or any other hapless souls targeted in the bloodbath. They became nothing more than prey, and were simply butchered without an iota of compunction.

Father Bernhard Stempfle of the Hieronymite Order was found in a forest near Harlaching, an affluent Münich suburb where Hess maintained his residence. Father Stempfle's neck was broken and he had been shot three times through the heart. His sin was that he knew too much about Hitler's affair with Geli Raubal. Prior to the girl's death in 1931 he had been instrumental in squelching a letter containing "coprophilic inclinations" written by Hitler and intended for Geli. To allow Father Stempfle further life was considered an unnecessary risk.

Not by the wildest stretch of the imagination could Dr. Wilhelm Eduard Schmidt have been labeled a threat to anyone. The well-known music critic for a Münich daily newspaper was playing the cello in his study while his wife prepared dinner. The peaceful scene was disrupted when SS men burst into the home, placed him under arrest, and spirited him away before the anguished eyes of his wife and three children. As he was being taken from his residence, Dr. Schmidt assured his family that he would return as soon as the obvious mistake had been rectified. In a few days he did return—in a sealed coffin. He had met a ghastly death by torture, and his family was not permitted to view the body. He had been killed in error, apparently mistaken for someone with a similar name who was a friend of Otto Strasser.

Even as the killings continued, Göring appeared at a press conference in the afternoon. Göring made a dramatic entrance and announced to the assemblage that a mutiny by Röhm and the SA had been successfully quelled. He added that former chancellor Kurt von Schleicher had been in on the plot to seize control of the government, and that he had "unfortunately" been shot and killed when he resisted arrest.

Konrad Adenauer. Taken into custody by the Gestapo during the Night of the Long Knives, he survived to eventually become Germany's first postwar Chancellor.

Louis Lochner, chief of the Associated Press Bureau in Berlin, rushed to his office and started dictating the story to London by telephone. He was cut off while he was into his final sentence. Lochner was the only correspondent to get through to the outside world that day.

Göring, of course, did not tell the whole story, as the murders continued unabated. Many of the victims were interrogated by Heydrich at Gestapo headquarters as he tried to extract every possible bit of information from them before they were silenced forever. The mounting death toll included outspoken lawyer, editor, and journalist Dr. Fritz Gerlich, who sought to discredit Hitler. Also, Fritz Beck, Director of the Münich Students' Welfare Fund. Doctor Voss, who had the misfortune of being Gregor Strasser's lawyer. Walter Schott, a journalist who had written a book about the Nazis that was too truthful in content. Dr. Karl-Gunther Heimsoth, the recipient of Röhm's careless homoerotic letters from Bolivia. Herr Glaser, an attorney who opposed Hans Frank. Chief of Police Ramshorn of Gleiwitz. Chief of Police Schräg-muller of Magdeburg. Erwin Villain, who knew too much abut the Reichstag fire. A number of other individuals who had knowledge of the fire were also liquidated before the homicidal wave spent itself. In Hitler's Germany, knowledge was a dangerous thing.

One intransigent who escaped with his life was Gerhard Rossbach, who had headed the Rossbach Freikorps. He had left Hitler after the Beer Hall Putsch and had been critical of both Göring and Hitler. Although arrested, he somehow managed to survive. After World War II he operated an import-export business in the Frankfurt area.

Himmler's predecessor as chief of the Gestapo was also slated for extinction, but at the last minute the name

Stadelheim Prison, as it looks today on Munich's Stadelheimer Strasse, where Ernst Röhm was executed in Cell 474 while many of his SA officers were slaughtered in the courtyard.

of Rudolf Diels was removed from the list by Göring, much to the displeasure of Heydrich. The Gestapo office in Cologne was not notified of the deletion, but Diels, an accomplished survivalist, had been warned and went into hiding for several days on a secluded estate in the Eifel Mountains. He did not reappear until danger had passed.

The setting sun had transformed the western sky into an eerie red palette late Saturday afternoon when Hitler flew back to Berlin. He met Göring and Himmler at the airport. A guard of honor was there to present arms. Hans Bernd Gisevius was at the Templehof Airport and observed that Der Führer was "pale, unshaven, and sleepless." The last person to appear at the open door of the aircraft was the grinning Göbbels, who had made it a point to stick close to Hitler during the killing spree. Himmler had in his hand a long list of names, which Hitler took from him and carefully scrutinized.

Theodor Eicke. Hitler gave Eicke complete control over all concentration camps.

Most of the people on the murder manifest had been slain by the following afternoon, Sunday, July 1, at which time Hitler was host at a tea party in the gardens of the Berlin Chancellery. It was a bizarre climax to an incredible weekend. For several hours Hess had been trying to elicit execution orders on Röhm, who was still alive in Münich's Stadelheim Prison. Finally Hitler made the decision.

While Hitler bantered with his guests at the tea party behind a façade of civility, captors placed a pistol loaded with a single bullet on a table in Röhm's cell. He contemptuously ignored the firearm.

"If Adolf wants to kill me," he told his tormentors, "let him do the dirty work!"

Ten minutes later, SS Officers Michael Lippert and Theodor Eicke appeared, and as the embittered, scar-faced veteran of Verdun defiantly stood in the middle of his cell stripped to the waist, the two SS officers riddled his body with revolver bullets. He fell to the floor, moaning "Mein Führer, mein Führer."

Operation KOLIBRI, which had started with Röhm's arrest in the tranquility of Bad Wiessee, was about to run its course, though at Lichterfelde Barracks the carnage before the red brick wall persisted. The citizens who lived in the immediate area heard continual gunfire for the rest of the day.

On orders from Göring and Himmler, all records connected with the mass murders were destroyed. On Monday the following message was transmitted over the police teletype system:

From the Prussian minister-president and the chief of the secret state police. To all subordinate police stations: All documents concerning the action of the last two days are to be burned, on orders from above. A report on the execution of this order is to be made at once.

As a result of this directive, the total number of purge victims will never be known. The figure in all likelihood exceeded one thousand. The list was indeed extensive. There are no photographs, no documents, no reports, nothing—except remembrance of the survivors and perpetrators.

Chapter 14

THE AFTERMATH

There was never any evidence to substantiate Hitler's contention that an actual coup was imminent in June 1934. What *had* existed—quite understandably—was considerable dissatisfaction with the new chancellor's harsh methods of governing, and, as always, an abundance of muttering and political intrigue.

As freedom of expression began to evaporate, many Germans were concerned about Hitler's increasingly repressive measures. Moreover, many SA leaders felt that Hitler no longer needed them and was looking for an excuse to jettison them as an encumbrance. Röhm had resented being shunted aside, and to counteract what he considered ingratitude—and duplicity—on the part of Hitler, he had entered into a secret agreement with Dutch oil magnate, Sir Henry Deterding. Under the deal, if Röhm had succeeded Hitler (with Deterding's financial support), Röhm would have given Deterding control of Germany's oil market. To further roil the waters, there were factions in Germany that favored restoration of the monarchy, with perhaps Crown Prince Rupprecht. It was against this backdrop that Hitler made his decision to move before various intrigues developed into something tangible. In reality, Hitler was the conspirator, and his intended victims had no idea what he had in store for them. What he needed was an opportunity and propitious timing.

Until he was arrested in March 1933 and subsequently sent to Dachau, Dr. Fritz Gerlich, editor of the anti-Nazi newspaper *Der Gerade Weg* (The Straight Way) had been doing all he could to undermine Hitler's regime. Gerlich, an implacable Nazi opponent, had totally discounted the explanation that Geli Raubal committed suicide, and darkly suggested that Hitler himself had something to do with her death. Working with journalist Georg Bell, Gerlich uncovered some of the details of the Röhm/Deterding agreement. Also, they had information that an SA leader named Julius Uhl had been designated triggerman to eliminate Hitler—if the nebulous scheme could be finalized—so that Röhm could supplant Der Führer. In a whirlwind of betrayals, Uhl shot Bell who had fled to Austria when Gerlich was arrested, and Uhl and Gerlich both ended up in Dachau where they were executed on July 1, 1934, during the killing spree.

The wily Göbbels may have been playing both ends against the middle. As late as the third week in June he had long and clandestine meetings with Röhm in the Bratwurstglöckl. The proprietor, Herr Zehntner (who had refuted Hitler's story in the Geli Raubal case), as well as the head waiter and the wine steward, were among those murdered during the weekend of terror. They were witnesses Göbbels had to eliminate once it became evident Röhm was destined to be the loser in the clash of wills with Hitler.

To citizens not touched, there was little or no objection throughout the Fatherland. AP Chief Lochner sent two of his German reporters out to interview Berliners, seeking views of "people in the street." The overall reaction was one of nonchalance—but not so with the Reichswehr. Officers of the Regular Army were pleased to see the SA leadership decimated. Major General Erwin von Witzleben remarked that he regretted he could not have personally witnessed executions of the SA victims. Ten years later, as a field marshal, he would himself be executed for complicity in a real plot—the attempt to kill Hitler with a bomb on July 20, 1944. He met an agonizing end at Plötzensee Prison, dangling from a meathook, with piano wire wound around his neck.

On July 3, the puppet cabinet legitimized the unlawful acts with a statute that read: "The measures taken on June 30, July 1, and July 2, 1934, to thwart attempts at treason and high treason, are considered as essential measures for national defense." By edict the blatant murders had become "essential measures."

The next day, the Fourth of July, Ambassador Dodd and his family hosted a large reception at their residence, a rented four-story villa secluded at No. 27 Tiergartenstraße. The three hundred or so guests included the acclaimed violinist Fritz Kreisler and several newspaper reporters—including Louis Lochner. The atmosphere was subdued. In an attempt at gallows humor, Martha Dodd and her brother Bill welcomed new arrivals with the remark: "Oh, so you're still among the living?" German guests were not amused.

A badly shaken Bella Fromm circulated about, moving from one small group to another, where conversations were conducted in hushed tones. She noted that the air ". . . was filled with electric tension. The diplomats seemed jittery. The Germans were on edge." Her own sentiments were anything but pro-Nazi, and this was no secret. Had her name ever been on the list? If so, who had removed it? In recent months, with each passing day the hostile environment had intensified for anyone—Aryan or non-Aryan—who expressed any form of opposition to the Nazis. Anyone who knew anything about Hitler realized that he was audacious to the point of recklessness. But this audacious? Could he shock the conscience of the German people and defy world opinion and get away with it? KOLIBRI was essentially an all-Aryan operation, initiated by non-Jews against non-Jews. What was next? Who was next?

Göbbels denied the German public any media coverage of the widespread killings by the Gestapo and the SS; he even prohibited the press from carrying the obituaries of the deceased. A brief official release announced that Röhm had been removed as head of the SA and that five of his top aides had been executed for "debauchery." This was followed by an equally curt press release informing the populace that Röhm had also been executed for refusing to "accept the consequences of his acts."

Outside of Germany, the media response was generally one of revulsion, even based on the limited facts available at the time. On July 2 the *St. Louis Post-Dispatch* said:

> Hitler, like Robespierre, 'the incorruptible,' has begun to kill. He has sent his bullets against men who, former friends or not, aroused his fanatic moral conscience. Nazis now have begun to kill each other. But Robespierre

met the fate he dealt out to his enemies, and today Germany asks where, when and with whom will the killing stop. No invention of a fiction writer could equal the wildly improbable melodrama of the last forty-eight hours' events in Germany.

On July 3 *The Times* of London followed with:

What is ominously symptomatic of the present state of Germany is the savagery, the disregard for all the forms of law which are the indispensable safeguards of justice and which are sacrosanct in every modern civilized state. What is of still deeper significance is the indifference— even the complacency—with which this resort to the political methods of the Middle Ages is apparently regarded.

A neighbor of Gregor Strasser's family had occasion to meet one of Gregor's sons a couple of days after the purge, and he asked the boy for his thoughts on his godfather. The frightened youth could only answer: "He is still our Führer!"

One person who would not be cowed was the courageous Kate Eva Schmidt, widow of the Münich music critic who had been killed "in error." On July 7 she was visited by a Gestapo official named Brunner who told her the death of her spouse was a "regrettable accident," but he refused to answer the many questions she put to him. She declined to accept money offered on at least two occasions in the next few weeks. A Gestapo representative finally left a sum of money at her apartment, despite her protests, but when he left she took the money to the Brown House where she talked to Captain Fritz Wiedemann, who would become Hitler's adjutant in 1935. He advised her that he would attempt to obtain a widow's pension for her.

Frau Schmidt next received an intimidating telephone call from Himmler, who—in an arrogant tone—told her to accept the monies proffered by the Gestapo, warning her to "keep quiet about the matter." She hung up on him, and immediately notified Wiedemann of the call. On July 31, Hess came to her residence and attempted to pacify her by expressing sympathy and suggesting that her husband's untimely demise could be regarded as "the death of a martyr for a great cause." Subsequently, she received a letter from Hess, dated September 24, in which he absolved her late husband of any wrongdoing. She eventually was granted a monthly pension of 1,000 marks.

Dr. Erich Klausener's family was further traumatized when his ashes were returned to them in a cardboard box. His widow retained lawyers and tried to bring suit for damages against the state, but the time for judicial remedy in Nazi Germany had already passed into oblivion. The attorneys were confined in a concentration camp in Sachsenhausen until the litigation was withdrawn.

A young SS recruit, who was also a newspaper photographer for the House of Ullstein, was assigned the unenviable duty of shooting victims in the Gestapo cellar. When the wholesale carnage was over, he reappeared for work after an unexplained absence of several days—in a distraught condition. He finally broke down, and revealed that he had personally been involved in killing thirty-seven victims. He was haunted by the callousness of the executions and was tormented by remorsefulness. But he made the fatal mistake of talking about it, and as a consequence he soon joined the ranks of the missing, never to be seen again. Remorse was not an acceptable Nazi tenet.

The newspaper staffers knew what had happened, but it would have been suicide to report it.

Hitler addressed the Reichstag on July 13 and attempted to justify the slaughter by claiming he was forced to take protective measures in order to suppress a mysterious surprise "attack" by Röhm (who had been on holiday) and the SA, although by no means did he come close to disclosing the scope and true nature of the massacre. He had to take action, he explained, because:

> After having repudiated all doubts about the loyalty of the chief of staff [Röhm], after having given this man unwavering and loyal friendship for many years, I began having my doubts about him because of warnings—especially from my deputy Rudolf Hess—that I simply couldn't ignore any longer.

The chancellor at this time gave the German people an idea of what to expect from him. "Everyone must know for all future time," he warned, "that if he raises his hand to strike the state, then certain death is his lot."

This was one promise he did not break. Hitler received the following telegram:

> From the reports presented to me I realize that through your determined action and through the courageous intervention of your own person you have nipped in the bud all treasonable plots. You have saved the German people from grave danger. For this I express to you my profound thanks and my sincere recognition.
>
> With best greetings,
> *Von Hindenburg*

Once again Hitler had hoodwinked the old man.[1] He would not have to do it again, because on August 2, 1934, the aged and befuddled president died. The next step had already been planned, as Hitler immediately announced the unification of the offices of president and chancellor under the title of Führer and Reich Chancellor. Anticipating the demise of the eighty-seven-year-old von Hindenburg, Hitler's cabinet had in fact passed the unification law the previous day, using the authority vested in it by the enabling act the chancellor had rammed through the Reichstag the previous year.

All officers and enlisted men of the armed forces were required to pledge personal allegiance to Hitler with this oath:

> I swear by God this sacred oath, that I will render unconditional obedience to Adolf Hitler, the Führer of the German Reich and people, Supreme Commander of the Armed Forces, and will be ready as a brave soldier to risk my life at any time for this oath.

Within a week of Röhm's liquidation, the cache of arms he had been hoarding for his SA in contravention of the Versailles Treaty was made available to the Reichswehr. General Liese, the army's head of military supplies, could scarcely believe his good fortune when he inspected this windfall. The Reichswehr no longer had reason to fear the SA. In the wake of the purge, Hitler and his cabal continued making the necessary moves to cover their tracks

---

[1]There has always been some doubt that von Hindenburg actually initiated this telegram. There is a suspicion that the telegram was composed and sent by Otto Meissner, the President's Secretary of State, who was later rewarded by Hitler with the post of Minister of State. Meissner was, in effect, von Hindenburg's Chief-of-Staff, and a key player behind the scenes.

Dr. Otto Meissner

and solidify their position. The obedient Viktor Lutze, Hanover SA leader who had helped in the Bad Wiessee arrests, was named Röhm's replacement as Chief of Staff of the SA. But the Brownshirts were never a factor again in the Reich's power structure. In recognition of their performance in KOLIBRI, the SS was severed from the SA on July 20 and made an independent force under Himmler, directly responsible to Hitler. The compliant Oskar von

Hindenburg was rewarded with a promotion to major-general.

Although the SA had been removed as a threat, the Reichswehr continued to view the SS with a certain wariness, especially after what had happened to von Schleicher and von Bredow. When the Reichswehr agreed to terms in the secret meeting with Hitler aboard the *Deutschland*, they did not realize they would have to sacrifice two of their own generals in the deal. One of Ambassador Dodd's contacts in the SS divulged an incident that had been publicly hushed up, revealing the extent of distrust and hostility that prevailed between the SS and the Reichswehr.

The Reichswehr did not believe Göring's obviously fabricated version of von Schleicher's death, and conducted their own inquiry. Göring had offered the fanciful explanation that von Schleicher had been shot while "resisting arrest." The Reichswehr had obtained for review the SS files on the von Schleicher affair, and then refused to return them. Four SS men visited the major who had custody of the files at the Reichswehr Ministry on April 11, 1935. The SS representatives demanded at gunpoint that the major relinquish the von Schleicher folder, but the major surreptitiously pressed a hidden alarm button that summoned armed guards to his office. The startled SS intruders were disarmed, taken to the cellar, and shot. The Reichswehr then turned the tables on the SS by sending the ashes of the slain men to Himmler.

By combining the offices of chancellor and president in August 1934, Hitler now held the Sword of Damocles over any German who dared to contradict him. The terror unloosed on June 30 was but a precursor. If Hitler could do this to his own people, was it reasonable to expect him to change his course of conduct in the future when it came to dealing with the vanquished of neighboring countries? Five years later, on August 22, 1939, he told his army commanders:

> The victor will not be asked afterwards whether he told the truth or not. When starting and waging war it is not right that matters, but victory. Close your hearts to pity. Act brutally.

It was to be KOLIBRI all over again, but on a much larger and more frightening scale.

Hitler was disinclined to overlook the pettiest past affronts when it affected him personally, and when the Nazis moved triumphantly into Vienna in 1938, Reinhold Hanisch was promptly taken into custody. The man who had sold Hitler's artwork in the early years and had been arrested on Hitler's complaint in 1910 now found himself at the mercy of the Gestapo. According to Martin Bormann, a dubious source, the man who had vowed to "even the score" with Hitler committed suicide by hanging himself in his cell.

Otto Strasser survived by crossing the border in Austria in May 1933, but his sanctuary there would not last for very long. He became the Teutonic embodiment of Philip Nolan, the central figure in Hale's *The Man Without a Country*, as he managed to keep one step ahead of the Gestapo. He was a fugitive from his native land, continually looking over his shoulder. He knew that if he ever fell into the clutches of his brother's former secretary, he would suffer an agonizing death.

Strasser fled from Vienna to Prague, then to France, and on to Switzerland. He retraced his path to France, and eventually made his way to the safety of Canada, via Bermuda. After the war he returned to Germany, and tried

Otto Strasser's opposition to Hitler never wavered.

to reenter the political picture. He had to resort to court action to have his citizenship restored. He organized a movement called the League for German Revival, and then started a new party, the German Social Union, but met with little success. He had eluded KOLIBRI, but he could not escape the stigma of an early association with Hitler. Frustrated and disillusioned, he died in München on August 27, 1974, at the age of seventy-six.

When William E. Dodd left his post as head of the History Department at the University of Chicago in July 1933 to accept President Roosevelt's appointment as United States Ambassador to Germany, he anticipated that he would be back in Chicago within a year. The president, in a private meeting, told him that in order to offset the Nazi influence, "I want an American liberal in Germany as a standing example." Dodd had spent time in Germany as a young man prior to the First World War. He even received a doctorate in 1899 from the University of Leipzig, and thought he had some understanding of the German mentality. But he did not think the Nazis would last very long, and, like almost everyone else he had badly underestimated Hitler.

Dodd was on the scene as the bloodletting of June 30 began, but, strangely (for a historian), he did not seem to grasp the significance of what was happening, and he was not inclined to speculate as to Hitler's motives. He was an eyewitness to history, but his vision was obscured. In his daily diary, he introspectively asked himself the question: "Ought I to resign?" He stayed on until December 1937. He was sixty-eight years old when he returned to his homeland, and in less than four years he was dead. His experiences in Nazi Germany had been trying.

Dodd had fully expected Hitler's regime to crumble within a year. Instead, it took the combined might of virtually all of the world's powers to bring the dictator to his knees, and then only after an all-encompassing war that dragged on for almost six years.

The chronicle of Hitler and his henchmen is a welter of plots and subplots, subterfuge and treachery, which—if detailed—would fill the shelves of an immense library. But the 1934 blood purge is the one historical occurrence that established Hitler's position as absolute ruler over his people. His antagonists were reeling before him, and this was the coup de grâce administered with killer instinct. As a consequence, a deadly time bomb had been set into motion. It began ticking away, eventually detonating into World War II.

In this one incredibly brazen and sanguinary swoop, Hitler eliminated all meaningful opposition within the borders of Germany. Some have called it the Night of the Long Knives. Who would now dare stand in his way? The implacable Röhm had been effaced. All that remained of Gregor Strasser was handed to his widow in an urn bearing the number 16 by way of identification. In addition to the hundreds who perished in the purgation, many dissidents were placed in concentration camps. Some were later released. Others were not. Hitler was now master of Germany, Commander in Chief of the Armed Forces. To defy him was to court death.

The miracle of Dunkirk was only six years away. And then Pearl Harbor, the siege of Stalingrad, D-Day, and finally, the agony of Hiroshima and Nagasaki.

One man—Adolf Hitler—was the catalyst who, in one way or another, wrought it all. Japan had already embarked on a path of aggression in Manchuria and China. Their interests were mainly focused on the Pacific theater of operations, but with the signing of the Tripartite Pact in Berlin on September 27, 1940, there was a significant shift of military concernment. Combat options now expanded. Germany, Italy, and Japan had now joined hands in alliance. The agreement stipulated that Germany would come to the aid of Japan if that country were attacked. However, in March 1941 Hitler told Japanese Foreign Minister Yosuke Matsuoka that Germany would "take part in case of a conflict between Japan and America," meaning that Germany would enter the fray regardless of who threw the first punch. For the remainder of the year Hitler encouraged Japan to strike at Hong Kong and Singapore, and he repeatedly emphasized the point that he questioned America's will to fight and continually downgraded the capability of American armed forces as he sought to embolden Japan's war planners. On November 28, 1941, even as Japan's task force was en route to Hawaii, von Ribbentrop assured Japanese Ambassador, General Hiroshi Oshima, that Germany would "join the war immediately" should Japan become engaged in a war against the United States. There can be little doubt that Hitler's exhortations influenced Japan's overall strategy. Japan hit Hong Kong, the Philippines, Singapore—and Pearl Harbor. And, indeed, Hitler immediately declared war on America. The Second World War had materialized. How would the course of history—and the destiny of millions of lives—have been altered if he had been the victim rather than the perpetrator that fateful day of June 30, 1934?

Inviting conjecture is the alternative question: What would have been the result had Hitler granted Röhm's wish and made him Minister of Defense, entrusting strategy and implementation of war plans and military objectives to the former Reichswehr captain? Röhm, who was no saint, was nevertheless an experienced infantry combat officer and a professional soldier through and through.

His organizational skills were acknowledged even by his many enemies. If his counsel had been sought, would he have deterred the Nazi warlord? Röhm was basically a revolutionary, but internal revolution is one thing; waging war against the world is something quite different. Would he—could he—have been able to restrain Hitler's aggression and appetite for expansion? Would the sybaritic Röhm have been able to convince Hitler that Germany should have shrewdly maintained the status quo, assimilating what had been gained in early successes rather than risking calamitous defeat on the field of battle?

To hypothesize further, if Röhm had, on the other hand, agreed with Hitler and shared his grandiose dreams of large-scale military operations, would he have been in a position to prevent some of Der Führer's flawed decisions? Röhm's expertise in military matters may have dictated an entirely different approach. He doubtless would have recognized the folly of a winter campaign against the USSR and the hazards of a two-front war. Would he have stopped at Dunkirk? Would he have ordered advances (with catastrophic casualties) in the bitter cold of the eastern front when tactical withdrawal was the prudent and logical military alternative? What would have been the ultimate outcome had Hitler delegated battle strategy to Röhm?

Chapter 15

THE FINAL CURTAIN

The chief engineers of the purge all met an inglorious end.

The youngest—Heydrich—was the first to die. His role in KOLIBRI stamped him as a reliable and merciless part of Hitler's despotic system, and his star was rising as a result. It would be extinguished in Prague.

When Hitler cast covetous eyes toward the Sudetenland of Czechoslovakia, he told a huge crowd at the Sportpalast in Berlin on the night of September 26, 1938: "This is my last territorial demand." Three days later Prime Minister Neville Chamberlain of Great Britain and French Premier Edouard Daladier affixed their signatures to the capitulation known as the Münich Pact, and the Sudetenland (consisting of 11,000 square miles) was incorporated into the Reich. Emboldened by the lack of resolve displayed by Chamberlain and Daladier in the Münich meetings, Hitler began charting his next course. Inside of six months Czechoslovakia in its entirety was swallowed by the Nazis. Threatened with massive bombing by Göring's Luftwaffe and invasion by the poised German Army, the Czech government surrendered to Hitler's new demands, and on March 15, 1939, all of Czechoslovakia was annexed without a shot being fired.[1]

Hitler issued an official communiqué advising that the citizens of Czechoslovakia would now be "under the protection of the German Reich." This was a euphemism which meant they had lost their liberties. To assure "protection," in September 1941 Hitler named Heydrich the Acting Reich Protector of occupied Czechoslovakia, replacing the ineffective Baron Konstantin von Neurath. As was expected of him, Heydrich immediately instituted a program of repression. He declared a "state of emergency," and established a tribunal of three Gestapo officials to pass judgment on all arrestees. The result was over four hundred death sentences, and four thousand confinements. Hitler's definition of "protection" was now understood by all.

Heydrich's additional duties in Prague did not preclude him from setting up and chairing the infamous conference of January 20, 1942, in the Berlin suburb of Wannsee, where the objectives of the "Final Solution of the European Jewish Question" were delineated.

---

[1]The Luftwaffe had acquired a fearsome reputation as a result of being previewed and tested in the Spanish Civil War. At the Nuremburg trials, Göring testified: "With the permission of the Führer I sent a large part of my transport fleet and a number of experimental fighter units, bombers, and anti-aircraft guns; and in that way I had an opportunity to ascertain, under combat conditions, whether the material was equal to the task." A thoroughly intimidated Czech President Emil Hácha knew what to expect if he persisted in resisting Hitler's demands to surrender.

In early May 1942 Heydrich made a quick trip to occupied Paris, where he stayed at the Hotel Ritz, and then returned to Prague to resume work. His life was about to end. The Czech government in exile, headed by Eduard Benes, in London, had decided to assassinate him. Two members of the resistance movement, Jan Kubis and Josef Gabcik, volunteered for the hazardous assignment, and on December 28, 1941, they parachuted into Czechoslovakia from an RAF Halifax bomber. After scouting the daily route taken by Heydrich, they ambushed him on May 27, 1942, on the outskirts of Prague. Kubis rolled a bomb under Heydrich's open Mercedes sports car after Gabcik's Sten gun jammed. Heydrich sustained massive injuries when the bomb exploded, and lingered for several days before succumbing on June 4.

The reprisals for this death reached outlandish proportions. In Czechoslovakia, 1,331 Czechs were summarily executed (including over 200 women), and in Berlin, 152 Jews were killed to avenge the assassination. Heydrich's evil legacy extended beyond the grave. In an act reminiscent of the atrocity in the Belgian town of Louvain during the First World War, the avengers decided to teach the Czech people a lesson they would never forget. On June 9 an SS detachment (from the "Prinz Eugen" Division) under SS Hauptsturmführer Max Rostock surrounded the village of Lidice near Prague and, as retribution, the hamlet was completely obliterated. All of the adult males, 172 in number, were lined up and shot. Seven women were taken to Prague to meet the same fate. The remaining 184 women were deported to concentration camps, and the 98 children relocated. As a finale, through dynamite and fire, the town was razed. Later, on June 18, 1942, based on information furnished by a betrayer, the SS found the assassins, Kubis and Gabcik, along with over a hundred other members of the resistance movement, hiding in a church in Prague. The SS encircled the church and killed them all. The clergymen who hid them were also put to death. Nine years would pass before SS Hauptsturmführer Rostock received his punishment. He was hanged in August 1951 in Prague.

In April 1945 as Hitler awaited his fifty-sixth birthday, he could look back on a life of peaks and valleys. He had started out as an indifferent student in his youth, and had gone on to be a failed artist and then a Vienna street person. Next, he was a battlefield courier, a frustrated politician, a defeated revolutionist, and ultimately—through a bit of political legerdemain—the chancellor. An Austrian by birth, he had been accepted by Germans as their Führer. He had eliminated the scourge of unemployment by imposing military conscription in March 1935, removing Jews from the workplace by either killing them or placing them in concentration camps, and instituting an extensive rearmament program as he prepared for war. He had also turned the country into a charnel house as he guided it into the abyss and the "unprecedented catastrophe" predicted by General Erich Ludendorff in 1933. Finally, enmeshed in a war he could not possibly win, he stubbornly refused to quit and preserve what was left of an utterly devastated Germany. On March 19 Albert Speer, the Reich Minister for Armaments and War Production, told him that the war was irretrievably lost, something that had been obvious for a considerable period of time. Hitler's response: "If the war is lost, the nation shall also perish."

Fortunately for mankind, Hitler did not have nuclear capability at his disposal, for most certainly he would have used it wantonly and indiscriminately. That sobering conclusion is inescapable when you consider his words:

"We may be destroyed, but if we are, we shall drag a world with us—a world in flames." And that is exactly what he tried to do.

With the war lost, with absolutely no possibility of victory, he declined to even discuss capitulation. Instead of assuming responsibility for the debacle, he blamed his generals, his acolytes, and finally, the German people he had betrayed and led to disaster. In August 1944 Hitler told a meeting of Gauleiters: "If the German people was to be conquered in the struggle, then it had been too weak to face the test of history, and was fit only for destruction." And now, eight months later, with total defeat inevitable and imminent, he rejected any suggestion of surrender and continued to needlessly sacrifice what was left of his military forces. As the Russians closed in on Berlin, madness prevailed. Out on the streets German soldiers (many of them mere youths) were still being hanged or shot as traitors for refusing to die for a leader who was hiding in his underground bunker with his mistress and contemplating suicide. On May 17, 1921, Hess had directed a letter to Gustav von Kahr and, in a mockery of words, wrote:

> I know Herr Hitler very well because I speak with him every day and am closely associated with him. He has a rare, upright, and flawless character. He is kind-hearted, religious, and is a good Catholic. He has only one goal and that is his country's well-being.

Otto Strasser's assessment of this same person was:

> He hated without knowing love. He was drunk with an ambition that was utterly without moral restraint, and had the pride of Lucifer, who wished to cast down God from His immortal throne.

If Der Führer had any reservations about taking his own life, they probably evaporated on April 29 when he received word of the ignominious death of his Italian counterpart, Benito Mussolini. The egocentric, strutting "Duce" was arrested by partisans as he tried to flee into Switzerland wearing a German greatcoat and helmet. On April 28 he and his mistress, Clara Petacci, were riddled with bullets and then taken to Milan where they were put on display. They were hoisted by their feet from the girders of a filling station as a vengeful mob spat upon the corpses.

Hitler's own longtime mistress, Eva Braun, had joined him in the Berlin bunker at the Chancellery, and on the evening of April 28 he deigned to marry the woman whose existence had for many years been a well-kept secret from the German public. Göbbels, still the Gauleiter of Berlin, managed to locate a minor municipal official named Walter Wagner who was authorized to perform marriages. Wagner was summoned to the beleaguered bunker to unite Hitler and Eva Braun in matrimony. Following the brief ceremony, Wagner enjoyed a modest repast of a liverwurst sandwich, not realizing he had less than an hour to live. As he warily made his way from the bunker and down the Wilhelmstraße, he was felled by a Russian bullet. He had joined the long list of Hitler's victims.

The honeymoon for the bride and groom consisted of a suicide pact, which was consummated on the afternoon of April 30, 1945. While Eva swallowed cyanide, Hitler shot himself in the right temple with his Walther 7.65-caliber pistol. In accordance with their wishes, the bodies were saturated with gasoline and incinerated in the Chancellery garden above the bunker.

On September 15, 1992, television viewers in Moscow saw what was purported to be actual film of the scene

Eva Braun

when Red Army combat forces arrived on May 2, 1945. The film showed what was alleged to be Hitler's body in an unburned condition, fully clad in a uniform and laid out on an officer's overcoat on the ground in the yard of the Chancellery. A Reuters dispatch reported that "the footage appeared to be from KGB secret police archives." If authentic, this would, of course, contradict what is generally acknowledged to be the true circumstances surrounding Hitler's finality.

There are at least two plausible explanations for this seeming inconsistency. On May 2, 1945, several Russian counterintelligence teams invaded the Chancellery area, seeking bodies. One team discovered several bodies crammed into an oak water tank, one of which bore a resemblance to Hitler, and at first—erroneously—was thought to be Der Führer. In a bit of gruesomeness, the corpse was briefly put on display in the main hall of the Reich Chancellery. (This may have been the body shown on television.) The next day, May 3, the charred remains of Hitler and Eva Braun were uncovered in a crater in the Chancellery garden. Lieutenant-Colonel Ivan Klimenko (head of one of the search teams) delivered the two bodies first to Plötzensee Prison, and then on to the 496th Field Hospital in Berlin-Buch, where autopsies were performed on May 8, 1945.[2]

There is another more likely explanation. It is known that in the summer of 1946 a Soviet film crew reenacted the last hours in the bunker and, complete with kleig

---

[2]With the end of the "cold war," additional information has come to light. In 1992 Russian television journalist Ada Petrova was given access to a secret file (labelled 1-G-23) in the State Archives of the Russian Federation in Moscow, which revealed that the charred corpses of Hitler and his bride were dug up and reburied several times by the Soviets. One of the directors of that facility showed Petrova fragments of a skull which he said was all that remained of Adolf Hitler.

lights and other paraphernalia, filmed the scenes at the actual site, using a cast that included some of the original participants who were now Russian prisoners. Hans Baur (Hitler's pilot) and Heinz Linge (Hitler's valet) were among the "actors" in the spectral replay.

When the German formations had successfully moved eastward in the early stages of the USSR invasion, the Waffen-SS (armed SS) and Einsatzgruppen (action groups) killed indiscriminately, pursuant to combat policies espoused by Hitler. The dead were by no means limited to military opposition; civilian casualties were also high. Now that the roles were reversed and the Russians were hammering westward toward Berlin, the Red Army did the same to the Germans. If surrender was to be involved, Germans much preferred to give themselves up to American or British authority. Hitler's refusal to consider surrender and his decision to delay suicide until the Red Army was virtually at the front door of the Chancellery effectively deprived his personal staff of escape routes to the west where they would have received better treatment. As it was, most of them were captured by the Russians, with less than pleasant results. Hans Baur, for example, was a prisoner for ten years, during which time he was repeatedly interrogated and tortured. While in Russian custody, he suffered the agony of having a bullet-shattered leg amputated with a pocketknife. Despite all of this, he went to his grave without publicly criticizing Hitler.

With Hitler dead, his secretaries, Gerda Christian and Gertraud Junge, accompanied by Bormann's secretary, Else Krüger, did make it to the west—eventually. After leaving the bunker they were joined by a female telegraphist from the Chancellery. There are various versions of what happened to them before they reached the sectors controlled by the Allies. Former *Newsweek* Berlin

Bureau Chief James P. O'Donnell, while researching ma-
terials for his book, *The Bunker,* personally interviewed
fifty surviving bunker witnesses, including Gerda Christian. According to O'Donnell, the four women fell into the
hands of a group of Soviet soldiers who subjected them to
a brutal two-hour gang rape before releasing them.

Göbbels knew that he would be held accountable no matter
who took him prisoner. He decided to follow the example
set by his leader. Göbbels was the man who perpetuated the
symbol of Der Führer as the Messiah through his successful
propaganda apparatus. He had defined propaganda as "winning people over to an idea in such a penetrating and all-
encompassing way that they will accept the idea totally and
will never be able to escape the clutches." That he did his
job well can be attested to by the realization that even today,
there are diehards in unified Germany who adhere to the
belief that Hitler pursued the correct course.

As the Third Reich entered its death throes, Göbbels
echoed Hitler's disdain for the German populace by saying:

> All the plans of National Socialism, all its dreams and
> goals, were too great and too noble for this people. The
> German people are just too cowardly to realize these
> goals. In the east, they are running away. In the west,
> they set up hindrances for their own soldiers and wel-
> come the enemy with white flags. The German people
> deserve the destiny that now awaits them.

Göbbels had belatedly reached his zenith in July 1944
when Hitler appointed him Reich Commissioner for Total
Mobilization of Resources for War. He would now descend

to his nadir. The man who did so much to destroy freedom for his country now prepared to commit the ultimate barbarism: Before killing himself, he would murder his own children. He wrote a testament in which he said that,

[O]n behalf of my children, who are too young to speak for themselves, but who would unreservedly agree with

Magda and Paul Joseph Göbbels posing with two of their six children, whom they would later murder.

Albert Speer professed to have no inkling of Hitler's plans for the extensive killing spree.

this decision if they were old enough, I express an unalterable resolution not to leave the Reich capital, even if it falls, but rather, at the side of the Führer, to end a life which will have no further value to me if I cannot spend it in the service of the Führer, and by his side.

The defenseless children, indeed, could not "speak for themselves," nor could they protect themselves from the twisted mind of their father. There were six Göbbels children—five girls, one boy—ranging in ages from four to twelve. Their first names all began with the letter H (as in Hitler). Up until the very last there was ample opportunity to evacuate the youngsters from what would soon become a chamber of horrors, but neither Göbbels nor his wife would hear of it. Albert Speer devised a plan to save the children, but the parents would not cooperate. Göbbels absented himself from the room when the children were poisoned, leaving the deed to his wife. She may have had help from her physician, Dr. Ludwig Stumpfegger, or SS Major Ludwig Kunz, who operated the Chancellery dental laboratory, but there was never any doubt as to who was making the decision. In the garden of the Chancellery, the parents of the dead children then reprised the Hitler/Braun rite. Göbbels shot himself in the right temple after administering the coup de grâce to his wife, who had bitten into her cyanide capsule.

■ ■ ▬ ─

Heinrich Himmler had proven his worth to Hitler in Operation KOLIBRI, and the former chicken farmer was rewarded as he rose to dizzying heights. He became the extermination specialist. He provided an insight into his thinking processes when, in a speech at Posnan on October 4, 1943, he told his SS officers:

> What happens to the Russians doesn't interest me; what happens to the Czechs, I find unimportant. That people are living in hunger and misery is only of importance to me to the extent that we need them as slaves for our culture. If 10,000 Russian women were to die of exhaustion while digging a tank ditch, it would be of interest to me only insofar as whether the tank ditch would be finished for Germany. . . . I also want to speak frankly to you about a most serious business. Among ourselves we must speak openly about it, although in public we will remain silent. . . . Every party member says that the Jewish people must be exterminated. That is clear, it is a part of our program. Good, we shall do it. This is a glorious page in our history.

By war's end Himmler had become Reich-Führer SS, Head of the Reich Police, Minister of the Interior, Commander in chief of the Replacement Army, and Commander of the Army Group Vistula. General Heinz Guderian, Chief of the General Staff, reacted with consternation when Hitler put Himmler in charge of actual fighting units at the battlefront. In Guderian's opinion, Himmler was totally unqualified for such an assignment, and he wrote ". . . the man inevitably proved a failure. It was a complete irresponsibility on his part to wish to hold such an appointment; it was equally irresponsible of Hitler to entrust him with it." Inexperienced in military matters and unable to cope with logistics, Himmler was relieved of his command of Army Group Vistula on March 20, 1945. One month later, April 20, he was at the Chancellery to help observe Hitler's fifty-sixth birthday. It was the last time they would see each other.

Now that all was lost, Himmler's self-preservation instincts surfaced. He unsuccessfully attempted to negotiate a surrender with the Western Allies, and when the BBC broadcast a Reuters dispatch on April 28 that Himmler had secretly contacted Count Folke Bernadotte of Sweden with the thought of surrendering German forces to General Dwight D. Eisenhower, the news was received in the bunker with disbelief and unbridled anger by Hitler.

Himmler was living in a dream world, driving around the Flensburg area in his Mercedes, accompanied by an entourage of SS men. He harbored the illusion that if he had an opportunity to personally confer with Eisenhower, he could persuade the Supreme Commander of the Allied Expeditionary Forces to join combat units with Germany to repel the Russians who were rapidly approaching from the east. He told an incredulous Albert Speer:

> Europe cannot manage without me in the future either. It will go on needing me as Minister of Police. After I've spent an hour with Eisenhower he'll appreciate that fact. They'll soon realize that they're dependent on me— or they'll have hopeless chaos on their hands.

When he finally faced reality and recognized the utter futility of his plan, he shaved off his moustache, donned an eye patch, and made his way toward the Elbe River, with false identification in his pocket. His small band had to abandon their vehicles at the Elbe, where they were ferried across in a fishing boat. The man who had ordered helpless men, women, and children to death camps in boxcars was now hiding and sleeping in peasant farms to escape detection.

He was captured by the British on May 23, 1945, between Hamburg and Bremerhaven, when (attired in an army private's uniform) he tried to slip through a control point. When his identity became known, he was initially interrogated and searched by Captain Tom Selvester, who found two small brass cases on his person. One case contained a cyanide capsule. The second case was empty, causing Selvester to suspect that Himmler had concealed an additional capsule. The prize prisoner was questioned again later that evening by Colonel Michael Murphy, General Montgomery's Chief of Intelligence, who also suspected that Himmler had the poison capsule secreted somewhere. A British Army physician, Captain C. J. L. Wells, arrived to assist in the examination. They stripped the prisoner, and searched his body, and when Dr. Wells ordered him to open his mouth, Himmler turned his head and bit into the hidden vial of potassium cyanide as the medical officer tried to put his fingers into his mouth. He was dead in twelve minutes. He was photographed, and a death mask made. The corpse was then wrapped in army blankets, trussed with telephone wire, and dumped into an unmarked grave dug near Luneburg.

Hermann Göring last saw Der Führer on Hitler's birthday on April 20, 1945, in the Berlin underground bunker. It was more like a wake, as the Reich Marshal—an exalted title that Hitler created especially for Göring in 1940—joined others in extending felicitations to the stooped Führer, who desultorily moved about the subterranean rooms. Bidding farewell to Hitler, he returned to the safety and comfort of his Berchtesgaden home. Three days later, he was visited by Luftwaffe General Karl

Koller, who notified him that Hitler was planning suicide. To Göring this meant that the law of succession should be invoked. This decree (last revised by Hitler on June 29, 1941) read that Göring should succeed Hitler if the latter should be "restricted in my freedom of action," or "if I should be otherwise incapacitated."

Göring was on the horns of a king-sized dilemma. He did not want to give the impression of usurping the Führer's authority, but he also did not want to forfeit the golden opportunity of becoming the number-one man in the Reich with the chance to endear himself to the Allies by negotiating an immediate cease-fire. After agonizing over the decision, he finally sent a carefully worded message to Hitler, asking, "Do you agree that I shall take over the leadership of the Reich as your deputy in accordance with the law of 29.6.1941?"

For Göring, the results were totally unexpected. Upon receipt of the telegram, Hitler flew into a rage. Encouraged by Bormann, who unbelievably had his own designs on the chancellorship, Hitler responded with a return wire accusing Göring of high treason, and requesting his resignation; then he simultaneously rescinded the existing law of succession. Bormann followed this up by dispatching an order to SS commanders at Berchtesgaden for Göring's arrest. The startled creator of the Gestapo was now getting a taste of his own medicine. He was taken into custody, placed in a room at Obersalzberg above Berchtesgaden, and not permitted to see his wife. While he was so confined, Lancaster bombers of the RAF, escorted by U.S. Mustangs, appeared overhead and demolished the Berchtesgaden retreats of Göring, Hitler, and Bormann, as well as the adjacent SS barracks, forcing everyone to flee to the protective bunkers nearby.

Twenty-seven years earlier, as commander of the Richthofen Flying Circus, Göring had experienced the collapse of the German High Command, and had disobeyed an order to surrender to American forces. Now, at the advent of Hitler's death and the resultant confusion in lines of authority, he became the beneficiary of a similar breakdown. Amidst the turmoil that followed Der Führer's suicide, he became a free man—temporarily. This time he would eagerly seek to deliver himself to those same Yanks. He wanted no part of the Russians.

In one of his final official acts, Hitler appointed Admiral Karl Dönitz as his successor with the title of President of the Reich and Supreme Commander of the Armed Forces. On May 6 Göring directed a message to Admiral Dönitz strongly suggesting that he should be utilized as a negotiator to meet with General Eisenhower. Dönitz did not even reply. Like Himmler, Göring seemed to think that he was the logical person to deal with Eisenhower, but the American general had already made the decision not to meet separately with any of the beaten Nazi representatives. Göring persisted by sending another message to Eisenhower, asking for a "man-to-man" interview, and he then sat back to await results. There were none.

On May 8 he decided to take matters into his own hands, and in the manner of a potentate on holiday he made his way toward the approaching Americans, with his entourage and forty-nine suitcases, some of which contained large quantities of paracodeine pills (his daily consumption now averaged one hundred tablets). He was found by First Lieutenant Jerome N. Shapiro of the United States Army between Mauterndorf and Fischhorn. Shapiro took him to Brigadier-General Robert J. Stack of the 36th Division at Zell-am-See. From there he was taken to the headquarters of the American Seventh Army at Kitzbühl, where he met with American General Carl Spaatz. Göring requested an audience with Eisenhower, and was confident it would be granted. It never happened. In fact, when Eisenhower learned of Göring's gentlemanly treatment, he became incensed and ordered that the Nazi leader be treated like any other prisoner of war. There would be no further favors. The Allies transferred him by air to the Seventh Army interrogation center at Augsburg, where he was shorn of his medals and his marshal's baton.

He was moved again on May 21, this time to Mondorf, where for the next four months the deflated Reich Marshal sat confined under guard at the Palace Hotel, an interrogation center for Nazi chieftans. It was here that he renewed his acquaintances with Robert M. Kempner, the prosecutor he had so insolently fired when he first took over as Prussian Minister of the Interior in 1933. Kempner, to Göring's discomfiture, was now acting in the capacity of official interrogator for his captors. Kempner had become an American citizen and would prove to be an invaluable member of the prosecution team in the forthcoming trial.

September 1945 found Göring behind bars at Nuremberg Jail, awaiting trial as a war criminal before the International Military Tribunal at the Nuremberg Palace of Justice. The precedent-shattering trial would last 217 days. During the course of the proceedings, he maintained his arrogance and repeatedly attempted to intimidate his co-defendants, on one occasion berating Albert Speer for acknowledging culpability. The former architect and Nazi War Production Minister, however, was not cowed by Göring, whom he called "a corrupt coward."

On the witness stand, nevertheless, Göring was impressive. In several sharp exchanges he clearly bested Robert H. Jackson, the Chief American Prosecutor, an

Robert H. Jackson at the Nuremberg Trials

Associate Justice of the United States Supreme Court, whose forté was not trial law. When Göring testified, he denied all crimes with which he had been charged, challenged the legality and jurisdiction of the tribunal, professed loyalty to Hitler, and—incredibly—averred that he had not been responsible for a single murder. Defiant to the end, in his final statement to the tribunal he said: "I never decreed the murder of a single individual at any time, nor decreed any of the atrocities, nor tolerated them while I had the power and the knowledge to prevent them."

So much for the credibility of the man who sat in the study of his Prime Minister's Palace in the Leipzigerstraße on a summer day in 1934 and—while munching sandwiches and quaffing beer—cavalierly dispatched his victims to the wall at Lichterfelde Barracks.

Göring's counsel called several witnesses to testify in his behalf. There was one notable absentee. Bruno Lörzer refused to appear as a witness for his former Luftwaffe chief.

On October 1, 1946, Hermann Wilhelm Göring heard the verdict: Guilty on all counts (conspiracy, crimes against peace, war crimes, and crimes against humanity). The punishment: death by hanging. His request for an alternative mode of execution—a firing squad—was rejected. It was the end of the line.

On October 7 he was visited by his second wife, Emmy, whom he had married in 1935. The vain peacock of the Third Reich had been a corpulent 280 pounds when he shook hands with Brigadier-General Stack. Now, seventeen months later, his ill-fitting Luftwaffe uniform, sans insignia, hung from his gaunt frame. Handcuffed to an American military policeman, he stared somberly past the partition separating him from his spouse in the interview room.

During his halcyon days Göring had reveled in ostentation and once told General Heinz Guderian: "How I love opulence!" When his first wife, Karin, died in 1931, he ordered for her grave in Sweden a massive pewter sarcophagus, large enough to hold both Karin and himself. In later years he appropriated a vast hunting preserve some fifty miles northeast of Berlin where, at considerable government expense, he built an enormous feudal manor which he called Karinhall. There he erected an ornate lakeside mausoleum, with five-foot walls of Brandenberg granite. A special train delivered the sarcophagus from Sweden to its new home. Ten days before the Night of the Long Knives, in an imposing service attended by Hitler himself, Göring re-interred Karin in the mausoleum where he expected to someday rest in regal repose next to his first wife. It did not work out that way. Instead, stripped of authority and privilege, he had been reduced to a suicidal death-row inmate, awaiting the inevitable.

On October 15, 1946, two hours before his rendezvous with the hangman, he bit into a vial of cyanide. Like Ernst Röhm and Gregor Strasser, he died in his cell. The question of how Göring came into possession of the lethal capsule—despite elaborate precautions—has never been satisfactorily answered. There are several theories. Among them: He somehow managed to conceal the capsule on his person or in his cell. It was hidden in his meerschaum pipe, which was always with him. It was surreptitiously slipped to him by an unknown person. A prime suspect was Dr. Ludwig Pflucker, a German urologist who had been given the assignment of looking after the Nuremberg prisoners. He was Göring's last visitor. The mystery remains unsolved.

There is yet another puzzlement to the story. Oddly, researchers had been unable to find an official record of the disposition of the bodies of Göring and his ten co-defendants, who were hanged. Over the years historians have speculated that the corpses were incinerated in the ovens at Dachau which—if true—would have been the height of irony. Now it seems that the most plausible final act was that they were cremated by a Münich undertaker and unceremoniously dumped in an estuary of the Isar River. Captain Gehrt would have approved.

Chapter 16

QUESTIONS

Of the Third Reich's "upper crust," the first to exit the corridors of power—and the last to die—was Hess. Although the schizophrenic Deputy Führer was the original "detail man" for Hitler, he gradually became disenchanted with details, which he frequently delegated to his ambitious underling, Bormann. While Hess was out skiing, hiking, flying, or racing his Mercedes, Bormann eagerly took over. But Hess was a troubled man. He had difficulty sleeping, and became a health faddist as well as a hypochondriac. The aftereffects of Operation KOLIBRI added to his torment. His physician, Dr. Ludwig Schmitt, later revealed that "on one occasion in my office, Hess broke down and wept over Röhm's death, blaming himself for it," because he had insisted on the SA leader's execution.

About 2:30 on the afternoon of May 10, 1941, Hess
had tea with his wife in their villa at 48 Harthauserstraße
in the wealthy suburb of Harlaching near Münich. After
kissing her hand, he departed with the remark that he was
uncertain as to the precise day of his return. He proceeded
to the Messerschmitt company airfield at Augsburg, where
he took off in a Messerschmitt 110 fighter plane, bound
for Scotland. The secret solo flight created an international furor and sent Hitler into another of his periodic
rages.

Hess flawlessly piloted the twin-engine craft nine hundred miles to the western coast of Scotland, eluding a lone
RAF Spitfire. Ironically, about the precise time he arrived
over Scotland, a massive Luftwaffe bombing raid killed or
injured approximately three thousand Londoners. The
Deputy Führer bailed out near Glasgow, where he was
taken into custody by astonished authorities. Hess insisted
on seeing the Duke of Hamilton, whom he had met at the
1936 Berlin Olympics. It was to the Duke that he first revealed his true identity after telling him that he had flown
to Scotland to arrange a peace settlement. The perplexed
Duke then flew to a site near Oxford where he personally
advised Prime Minister Churchill of the peculiar development. The "settlement" Hess proposed would leave Europe to the Germans and most of the British Empire to
Britain. (The Soviet Union's dictator, Josef Stalin, always
suspected that the purpose of the Hess flight was to neutralize Great Britain so that Hitler would have a free hand
invading Russia.)

Richard II, Henry VI, and Sir Walter Raleigh were
some of the personages who had been held prisoner in the
Tower of London. The name of Rudolf Hess would now
be added to the long list of prisoners confined in that sto-
ried structure. On May 17, 1941, he was transported to

the Tower on the banks of the Thames, but his residency there was short-lived. While Sir Walter had been an unwilling guest for thirteen years, Hess spent a mere four days there. But what he did not know was that he would never enjoy another moment of freedom.

Hitler ordered a statement issued, labeling Hess as a person suffering from "a mental disorder." Hitler made it clear that Hess's bizarre flight and mission were undertaken without his knowledge or approval. Rebuffed as a self-appointed peace emissary, Hess was interned by the British as a prisoner of war. On May 20 he was taken to Mychett Place, an old Victorian-style mansion south of London at Aldershot, a British Army base. Isolated under close guard, this was his home for the next year. In June 1942 he was again transferred, this time to Maindiff Court, a hospital at Abergavenny in South Wales.

The stubborn Hess proved to be a most troublesome prisoner for the British. He continually complained about his food, his living quarters, his medical treatment. He was obsessed to the point of paranoia with the fear that he would be poisoned. He twice attempted suicide, but there was some question as to whether he actually meant to take his own life or, instead, merely intended to draw attention to himself. While at Maindiff Court he realized what lay ahead for him: trial as a war criminal. He began his defense strategy by feigning amnesia. On October 8, 1945, he went to Nuremberg to join his codefendants. He was back in Germany, but scarcely in surroundings he could have envisioned when he bade his wife farewell four years earlier.

Upon arrival at Nuremberg he was taken to a small stone cell in the prison block adjacent to the Palace of Justice. When he made a complaint, he was curtly told that he was now in the custody of the Americans—not the

British. The day after his arrival he was ushered into the office of Colonel John H. Amen, chief of the Interrogation Division, where he was confronted with fellow prisoner Hermann Göring. Continuing his pretense of memory loss, he asked the former Luftwaffe chief: "Who are you?"

Göring considered Hess's amnesia as nothing more than a ruse, and, anxious to escape the confines of his own cell for at least a brief interval, he volunteered to expose his ex-confederate in a private conversation. Accordingly, on October 15 the two former Nazi bigwigs were put in a room together, the door closed, and a recording secretly made of the strange question-and-answer session. Hess, who knew all about surreptitious recordings, was not to be fooled. After more than an hour of futile efforts, an exasperated Göring gave up.

The much-awaited trial opened on November 20, 1945, with worldwide media coverage. Ten days later there was a break in the proceedings as Hess's attorney, Gunther von Rohrscheidt, argued that his client was not competent to stand trial and could not assist in his defense because of his memory impairment. After the lawyer had completed his lengthy presentation, however, Hess stood up and removed a prepared statement from his pocket and read it to the tribunal. The deception was over. To the chagrin of his lawyer—and several psychiatrists who had been duped—Hess admitted that his amnesia had been faked and that he was now ready to stand trial with the other defendants, although he still challenged the right of the tribunal to judge him. In his statement, he said:

> The reasons why I simulated amnesia are of a tactical
> nature. In fact, only my ability to concentrate is slightly
> impaired. On the other hand my ability to follow the

> trial, to defend myself, to question witnesses, and to
> answer questions myself—these are not impaired. I em-
> phasize that I assume full responsibility for everything
> that I have done, everything that I have signed, and
> everything that I have co-signed. . . . I have successfully
> maintained the illusion of amnesia with my official
> defense counsel; he has acted accordingly in good faith.

The prosecution began presenting evidence against him
on February 7, 1946. There was considerable speculation
about whether he would testify in his own defense. He did
not. He did, however, make a final statement to the tribunal after all the evidence was presented by both prosecution and defense counsel, in which he reaffirmed his
loyalty to Hitler and added: "I do not regret anything."

On September 30, 1946, he was found guilty on two
counts—conspiracy and crimes against peace. His penalty:
life imprisonment. He had expected the death sentence.

In July 1947 Hess and the other convicted prisoners
were transferred to Spandau Prison in the western sector
of Berlin in the British zone. The man who is said to
have inspired the Nazi ideology of *Lebensraum* (living
space for Germans) was to spend over four decades confined in the forbidding 147-cell fortress. One by one his
fellow inmates were released until he was the only sur-
vivor, and for the last twenty-one years of his life he was
the sole occupant in a facility built to accommodate six
hundred prisoners. Each month there was a changing of
the guard, as the United States, Britain, France, and the
Soviet Union took turns watching him. Over the years
there were repeated efforts to obtain his release on hu-
manitarian grounds, but the Soviet Union (who wanted
him executed at Nuremberg) steadfastly refused to join in
any act of lenience. To pass the time he would feed the

birds in the prison garden, or watch television, including such programs as *Dallas* and *Dynasty*, although his sight was failing. In the beginning he was the beneficiary of Hitler's power. Eventually he became—as did so many others—a victim. There were reports that while at Spandau he again attempted suicide.

As a young flying enthusiast Hess had at one time harbored an ambition to emulate Charles Lindbergh's solo, nonstop flight across the Atlantic, reversing the Lone Eagle's route by crossing from east to west. Instead, he had answered the siren call of Hitler. So now, as an old man, the remorseless Prisoner Number Seven huddled in his cell, awaiting death, a haunting relic from the past, never wavering in his espousal of Nazi goals or his allegiance to Hitler. "I once served under the greatest man who was ever born under the sun," he defiantly told Lieutenant-Colonel Eugene Bird, the U.S. Army Spandau Commandant from 1964 to 1972.

In the end, Hess died as he had lived—enmeshed in controversy. On the afternoon of August 17, 1987, his American warder inexplicably left his ninety-three-year-old charge alone for a short interval in a small cottage at the garden's edge. When the guard looked into the cottage a few minutes later, he observed the crumpled, unconscious form of Hess with an electrical cord tightly wound around his neck. Rushed to the nearby British Military Hospital, he was pronounced dead at 4:10 PM. A suicide note, addressed to his wife, was found in his pocket.

An autopsy, performed at the hospital by Dr. J. Malcolm Cameron, professor of forensic medicine at London University, determined that death resulted from "asphyxia, caused by compression of the neck due to suspension." At the request of the dubious Hess family, a second autopsy was conducted in Münich by Dr. Wolfgang Spann, a forensic medical specialist, with the same general results. Despite unanswered questions, the official verdict remained unchanged: self-inflicted death. The body was buried in the Hess family plot at Wunsiedel. The reason for Spandau's existence expired with the demise of its final prisoner, and the aging, red brick building was razed.

"The Last Nazi," as Hess had often been termed, was gone, but not the controversy that always seemed to surround him. Did Hitler know of his plans to parachute into Scotland? The answer to that question may never be known, but Heinz Linge, Hitler's valet, was convinced that his boss knew in advance of Hess's plan of action, and that he put on an act worthy of a veteran thespian when he was told of his deputy's flight. Said Linge:

> It flashed through my mind that he had already had known. . . . to my own surprise I noticed that he only showed surprise, anger, or bewilderment in the presence of others. Perhaps he had known the exact moment that Hess had left. I could not help thinking about the more than four-hour meeting that Hitler and Hess had had on the Obersalzberg several days before the flight. The two of them had not had such a long meeting since before the war.

Persons who knew Hess well opine that he was so subservient to Hitler, he never would have planned or undertaken such a mission without Der Führer's knowledge and consent.

When it comes to Rudolf Hess, there is no shortage of speculation. There are several theories. One of the strangest and least credible is the contention of Dr. Hugh Thomas that the man prosecuted at Nuremberg and imprisoned at Spandau was not even Hess. Dr. Thomas detailed his argument in his book, *The Murder of Rudolf Hess*, published in 1979. The improbability of this scenario is evidenced by the fact that such former colleagues and codefendants as Göring, Speer, von Papen, and others would have recognized a double, and would have utilized this knowledge to help discredit the prosecution. Also, the Hess family quickly took possession of Hess's body after his death and buried it in the family plot, something they never would have done if they even remotely suspected an imposter.

On September 5, 1987, the French weekly magazine *Le Figaro* published an article by German historian Dr. Werner Maser, in which the author made the startling assertion that in early 1952 (during a month the Soviets were providing guards at Spandau Prison), Hess was secretly removed from the prison—without the knowledge of the Western powers—and flown to an unknown destination on orders from Stalin. Away from Spandau for just one night, Hess was offered immediate freedom if he would agree to assume leadership of East Germany. Dr. Maser revealed that this confidential information was personally given to him in May 1952 by Otto Grotewohl, a former head of the East German government, who died in 1964. According to Dr. Maser, Grotewohl told him:

> I was on the plane that carried him. On that night the Russians and their East German intermediaries proposed to him a contract. He would make a public proclamation saying that the socialism he had dreamed about all his life was being practiced in East Germany.
>
> If he did this, his captivity would end. Without returning to Spandau, he would be freed immediately and they would make available to him a home in an elegant residential neighborhood. . . . Hess categorically

refused, with arrogance, what was proposed to him. He said he could not play such a trick on Adolf Hitler after Hitler's death.

According to Dr. Maser (quoting Grotewohl), Hess was then returned to Spandau.

On June 10, 1992, the British government released additional documents from their Hess files, but added little to the historical record. What was not released was the mysterious File 371, No. 26565, from the first months of Hess's captivity. That is being retained by the government into the next century for unexplained reasons of "national security," according to the British Foreign Office. Why this particular file would still be kept secret is in itself a puzzlement. Another historian, John Costello, published a book in 1991 in which he claimed that Hess had been "lured" to England by false promises of peace.

So what is the true story of Hess, and what really precipitated his departure from Augsburg in May 1941? The answer is obscured in a phantasmagoria of fact, fiction, and conjecture. On the basis of available information, historians at this point simply don't know.

The person who profited most by Hess's flight from freedom to captivity was his chief aide, Martin Bormann. When Karlheinz Pintsch, adjutant to Hess, broke the news of the flight to Hitler at the Berghof (Hitler's residence at Obersalzberg, high above Berchtesgaden), Bormann backed away from Pintsch as though he were a pestilence carrier, pleading, "That's nothing to do with me. Don't involve me." On Hitler's orders, Bormann had Pintsch arrested on the spot.

With Hess out of the way, Bormann moved to the top as his replacement. He became Hitler's administrative assistant with the title of Director of the Party Chancery, and Führer's Secretary. He eventually supplanted all of Hitler's closest advisers who had seniority over him. He was loathed by all of the top-level Nazis, but they were powerless to do anything about it because he enjoyed Hitler's complete support and confidence. Hitler relied on him to the extent that he even appointed him executor of his will, and the compound at Obersalzberg was registered in Bormann's name.

"I know Bormann is brutal," Hitler conceded, "but there is sense in everything he does, and I can absolutely rely on my orders being carried out by Bormann immediately, and in spite of all obstacles Bormann's proposals are so precisely worked out that I have only to say yes or no."

Unlike Hitler and Göbbels, Bormann had no intention of sacrificing his life in the besieged Führerbunker in the waning days of April 1945. After unsuccessfully attempting to persuade Hitler to transfer his headquarters to his Berghof above Berchtesgaden, he started to plan his own salvation. With Hitler and Göbbels dead, the remaining occupants of the underground refuge began to scatter in all directions. Some survived. Others didn't. On the night of May 1, Bormann made his bid for freedom. "Well, then, good-bye," he said to his secretary, Else Krüger. "There's not much sense in it anymore. I'll have a try, but I won't get through." Whether or not he did was unclear at the time.

An inebriated Bormann left the bunker in a fifteen-man group that included Hans Baur and Dr. Stumpfegger. Baur lost track of Bormann an hour or so before daylight, and never saw him again. Statements by various members of Hitler's staff were hopelessly conflicted when describing the chaotic exodus into the debris-strewn streets of Berlin. Some said they saw Bormann dead, while others insisted they had seen him alive subsequent to the time

other survivors claim to have observed his lifeless body—
which was never found. SS Major Joachim Tiburtius, a
successful escapee, later said that he had encountered Bormann at a hotel in the nearby Moabit section and that
"We pushed on together, toward the Schiffbauerdamm
and the Albrechtstraße. Then I finally lost sight of him.
But he had as good a chance to escape as I had."

There was simply no conclusive proof that he had perished, and the prosecutors at Nuremberg took no chances.
He was tried and convicted in absentia—and sentenced to
death.

Subsequently, there were recurring rumors that Bormann had indeed escaped the flames of Berlin and had
made his way to South America. In May 1948, Nuremberg prosecutor Robert H. Jackson was intrigued when
he received a tip from an American in the import-export
business in Uruguay, indicating that Bormann might be
living in Argentina. Jackson was inquisitive enough to
ask President Harry Truman to authorize an FBI investigation into the matter. "Obviously," Jackson wrote to
the president, "the situation requires discreet handling."
That's not exactly the way it turned out. On June 21,
1948, Truman asked the FBI to examine the matter. An
unenthused J. Edgar Hoover sent a single agent, Francis
E. Crosby, to South America with orders to conduct a
"preliminary investigation," and that is precisely what he
did. The cursory, one-man inquiry accomplished nothing. Crosby was in South America from July 3 to August
23, but made no effort to contact United States Ambassador James Bruce in Buenos Aires, who was anxious to
assist and could have been helpful. The ambassador was,
in fact, unaware of the agent's presence in Argentina, and
did not find out about it until after Crosby's return to
Washington.

On January 21, 1949, the disgruntled Bruce sent a radiogram to the State Department, giving his views as to why the FBI investigation was unproductive. According to Ambassador Bruce's message, "the FBI agent was not very discreet and it soon became known what his mission was." This was at variance with Hoover's report to Justice Jackson, which justified closing the case by saying the agent had "made a thorough, intelligent, and adequate preliminary investigation."

On May 5, 1955, the Allies transferred further prosecution of Nazi war criminals to German authorities, and the pursuit of the Bormann affair was not one of their top priorities. Interest was resuscitated in November 1972 when a series of articles by Ladislas Farago appeared in the London *Daily Express* suggesting that Bormann was alive and residing in South America. The focus of attention shifted to Berlin the very next month when, during excavation work on a building site, the skeletal remains of two bodies were uncovered near the Lehrter train station. German officials announced that they had discovered the remains of Bormann and Dr. Stumpfegger. Identification was based on dental evidence. Dental charts for Dr. Stumpfegger—but not Bormann—were on file for comparison purposes. The chart available on Bormann was the one prepared—from memory—by Dr. Hugo Johannes Blaschke, formerly Chief of the SS Dental Corps. To help settle a dispute, a dental forensic expert, Dr. Reidar F. Sognnaes of UCLA was—after considerable delay—given permission to examine the partial remains. After a further delay of one year, he reported in September 1974 that, in his opinion, the skull was Bormann's.

There was another perplexing sidebar to the story. While researching material for a book on Dr. Josef Mengele, investigative lawyer Gerald Posner said that in a

1984 visit to Argentina, he saw a "one-foot-high file" on Bormann belonging to the Federal Police. He was not permitted to peruse the file. In November 1991, Argentine President Carlos Menem advised that police in his country *did* have a file on Dr. Mengele—but not Bormann. This contradicted an earlier statement from Foreign Minister Guido di Tella in which he acknowledged that such a file on Bormann did exist. If Posner did in fact see such a file, the question that logically arises is: If Bormann died in Berlin a few hours after escaping from the bunker in May 1945, why did the police in Argentina have a file on him? Understandably, speculation was widespread.

South America had become a haven for ex-Nazis after the fall of the Third Reich. The destruction and/or concealment of records by authorities there oftentimes thwarted efforts to track down fugitive war criminals who had escaped from Germany. Adolf Eichmann, Chief of the Jewish Office of the Gestapo, would never have been located or apprehended if searchers had to rely on cooperation of Argentine authorities. Eichmann was eventually found by Israeli secret agents in May 1960 in a suburb of Buenos Aires, abducted, and flown to Israel for trial on charges of crimes against the Jewish people and crimes against humanity. He was convicted and executed. Most historians subscribe to the belief that Bormann died soon after leaving the bunker and that the remains unearthed in Berlin are indeed those of Bormann. Whatever doubts remained were seemingly removed in May 1998 when results of DNA tests performed in Frankfurt were released. Blood samples from Bormann's surviving relatives were DNA-identical to specimens taken from the skeletal remains found near the Lehrter train station in 1972.

Bormann had been the consummate "company man," a relatively minor component in the machinery as Operation KOLIBRI callously annihilated its victims, setting into motion a sequence of events that would ultimately bring about the cataclysm of World War II. But through craft and guile he was destined to eventually become a major player. For years he had sought to undermine those he perceived as his rivals. One by one—in one way or another—they were all eliminated: Hess, Heydrich, Göbbels, Himmler, Göring. And then there were none. The master manipulator had survived them all. But for Martin Bormann, it was too late. The Third Reich had ceased to exist.

Chapter 17

RETROSPECT

In recapitulating the events of June 30 through July 1, 1934, an amalgam of impressions emerge. In Hitler we see a mass murderer at work, with all the elements of first-degree homicide: motive, intent, and premeditation. It has variously been called The Blood Purge, The Röhm Putsch, Operation KOLIBRI. Otto Strasser labeled it The German Saint Bartholomew, drawing an analogy to the two-day massacre of French Huguenots during the reign of Charles IX in 1572. But mostly it has been termed The Night of the Long Knives—despite the fact that the bulk of the killing took place during daylight hours, and guns rather than knives were the implements of death. By whatever name, it sealed Germany's fate.

In early 1934 an unbelievable level of intrigue swirled throughout the upper echelons of the German government. Rumors were rife, and with each passing month the animosity between the Reichswehr and the SA intensified. Hitler's penchant for pitting individuals and factions against each other had reached an uncontrollable level. His position as chancellor was becoming precarious, and he realized that his survival was uncertain. For the sake of speculation, the question might be asked: What would have happened if Hitler had been eliminated or sidetracked during this unsettling political mélange? Who would have supplanted him? Who *could* have? In 1934 a viable political leader who espoused a democratic-type government in Germany was indeed a scarce commodity. So, who—realistically—was in a position to replace Hitler had he in some way been shunted aside?

Franz von Papen and Kurt von Schleicher had already demonstrated their inadequacies during their brief stints as chancellor. Röhm was not to be seriously considered, since he was loathed by the Officers' Corp of the Reichswehr. The so-called "Deutschland Pact" was predicated both on Hitler's suppression of Röhm and on Reichswehr support for Hitler's succession to the presidency; it was common knowledge that the eighty-seven-year-old von Hindenburg was near death. During the purge the Reichswehr was ready, if called upon, to strike the SA; but as it turned out the Gestapo and the SS required no assistance in carrying out Hitler's orders. The Reichswehr would never have countenanced the elevation of Röhm to the chancellorship. So who was left? The most likely candidate would probably have been Gregor Strasser, who was the antithesis of the dysfunctional Hitler.

The forty-two-year-old Strasser, a good-humored family man, was one of the organizers of the original Nazi Party in the "old days," and was the recognized leader of the Left Wing of the party. He was always regarded as Hitler's chief rival within the ranks, but lacked Hitler's canny ability to exploit opportunities. Strasser matriculated at the University of München. His twin sons Helmuth and Gunther resulted from his marriage to his childhood sweetheart. To a large extent he was responsible for keeping the party afloat while Hitler served his sentence in Landsberg, and he represented the Nazis in the Reichstag. He and Hitler did not always agree on methods and goals, and the rift widened after Strasser was offered the post of vice-chancellor in 1932, by then-chancellor von Schleicher. During an unpleasant confrontation with Hitler, during which Strasser was accused of being a traitor, an embittered Strasser resigned all of his party posts and returned to the private sector in late 1932. He accepted a position as director for a chemical combine (Schering-Kahlbaum), earning more money than he had ever made in his life. He had assured his employer that he had withdrawn from the political arena, but if he had been tapped for the chancellorship, it is unlikely that this would have been a problem. He still enjoyed a following in party circles, and considerable stature. This is not to say that he was without political hindrances. He was an idealistic socialist who favored expropriation of banks and heavy industry, and harbored a strain of anti-Semitism, which, although mild when compared to Hitler's virulency, was still a factor. Whatever chance he had to redirect the course of the Nazi Party—and the destiny of Europe— died in a blood-soaked Gestapo cell.

It was no secret that Hitler had an intense dislike for lawyers, and as soon as he became chancellor he began taking steps to control the legal profession. His firm grip quickly tightened at the throat of the legal fraternity.

Fervent Nazi Hans Frank (hanged at Nuremberg) became Reich Minister of Justice, exercising authority over the admission of attorneys to the field of practicing law. In a report dated August 24, 1936, Martin Bormann advised Frank that Hitler "has decided that women cannot become either judges or lawyers." A law passed on 3 December 1935 required lawyers to swear an oath of loyalty to Hitler. If an attorney in Germany was reluctant to prostrate himself in this obsequious manner, he had only to think of what happened to Gerd Voss, Gregor Strasser's lawyer, who was shot dead in his office (the same day his client was killed) when he refused a demand to open his safe. Or the untimely end of attorney Alexander Glaser who was felled by bullets just outside his door during the weekend bloodbath.

While all of this was happening, a young Albert Speer seemed oblivious to what was going on around him—or so he later claimed. He had become Hitler's architect after he joined the Nazi Party in 1931, became a favorite of the chancellor's, and ended up in 1945 at war's end as Reich Minister for Armaments and War Production, controlling all German production. He was an anomalous fit in Hitler's inner circle. He was urbane, educated, from a good family. In his memoirs, Francis Biddle, one of the American judges at the Nuremberg trials, wrote that Speer was "the most humane and decent of the defendants." Speer readily acknowledged his culpability in the affairs of the Third Reich, saying "I do not believe there can be any atonement in this lifetime for sins of such huge dimensions." Yet, oddly, he seemed to reflect a total indifference toward the savagery of the Night of the Long Knives. In his voluminous book, *Inside The Third Reich*, he hardly mentioned the 1934 wave of terror. While the book comprises 526 pages, Speer devoted scarcely three of them to the incident, furnishing scant details despite the fact that he was in

Berlin at the time and in frequent personal contact with Hitler.

In September 1966 Speer was released from Spandau Prison, having completed a twenty-year term imposed by the Nuremberg Tribunal after conviction on crimes-against-humanity charges and war crimes. He wrote the first draft of his book during his imprisonment at Spandau. In 1971 interviewer Eric Norden attempted to elicit from him his true feelings regarding the widespread killings. Speer admitted that he was close to Hitler during this period and that "the emerging pattern should have been clear to me."

Norden persisted: "Did the bloodiness of the purge repel you?" Speer replied:

> No, I hate to admit, it did not. Right after the purge, I was assigned to renovate the vice-chancellor's office in Berlin. When I entered Vice-Chancellor von Papen's office I saw a large circle of dried blood on the floor of one room where his aide, Herbert von Bose, had been shot to death by the SS. I instantly averted my eyes and from that moment on, I stayed away from the room. But that was the only effect the incident had on me; it was as if I'd drawn a curtain inside my mind, blocking the incident off. All I was concerned with in those days was my ambition to excel as Hitler's architect.

Years later it was Gitta Sereny, Speer's biographer, who tried to pin him down, but Speer again distanced himself from the event, claiming, "I didn't know about it ahead of time. People will never believe me or understand when I say this, but my mind was on other things."

After his release from Spandau, Speer fashioned a second career for himself as an author and authority on the

Third Reich. He died under embarrassing circumstances on September 1, 1981, while on a trip to London to participate in a BBC television documentary, titled *The Great Art Dictator.* He suffered a stroke in a room at London's Park Court Hotel while in the company of his mistress, to the chagrin of his wife and children in Germany. He was rushed by paramedics to St. Mary's Hospital in Paddington where he succumbed.

Even before Speer and his fellow defendants stood up before the tribunal at Nuremberg to learn their fate, Sepp Dietrich was brought before the bar of justice at—of all places—Dachau. He was captured by the American Seventh Army on May 9, 1945, and it would be a decade before he was again a free man. He was taken to Nuremberg on November 5, 1945, where he was to be a witness in the main war crimes trial of the Nazi big shots, but he never was called to the witness stand. Instead, on March 16, 1946, he was transferred to Dachau to join other SS personnel awaiting trial before an American Military Government Court made up of seven U.S. Army officers. The defendants were accused of shooting captured prisoners of war in several cases, including the infamous "Malmedy Massacre" in Belgium during the Battle of the Bulge. Despite his denial of guilt, Dietrich was convicted and on July 16, 1945, he was sentenced to life imprisonment. Ironically, he was incarcerated at Landsberg, the same prison where Hitler had been held when he wrote *Mein Kampf.*

Subsequently, after a series of appeals, Dietrich's sentence was modified, and he was released on parole on October 22, 1955. His freedom was brief. Belatedly, the postwar government of Germany decided to do something about the 1934 murders. In August of 1956, Dietrich and Michael Lippert were arrested for their role in the killing of Röhm and others at Stadelheim Prison. They were charged with manslaughter in a trial that began May 7, 1957, in Münich, the scene of the crime. Dietrich's defense was that he was merely following orders. Lippert tried to shift the entire blame to Theodor Eicke, who had been killed on the eastern front in 1943 after having been promoted to General of the Waffen-SS. Lippert claimed that it was Eicke alone who had shot Röhm, and that he was only an onlooker who had never even entered Röhm's cell. Lippert's version was contradicted by a police lieutenant who was an eyewitness to the shooting.

After a one-week trial both Dietrich and Lippert were found guilty and given eighteen-month sentences—and Dietrich found himself back in Landsberg Prison. The Chancellor of Germany at this time was none other than Konrad Adenauer, who had been arrested by the Gestapo within hours after his neighbors Elizabeth and Kurt von Schleicher had been slain. Due to deteriorating health, Dietrich was released in just six months. Unlike his luckless victims who crumpled before firing squads in Stadelheim Prison, he lived to die in bed at age seventy-four following a heart attack on April 21, 1966.

In addition to those put to death, hundreds of others were arrested and incarcerated for months, and even years. At Nuremberg, Field Marshal Erhard Milch said that in 1935, seven to eight hundred victims of the purge were still in Dachau. How many lives were snuffed out that weekend? We will never know. With all records and reports deliberately obliterated, and the press thoroughly intimidated, ordinary Germans had no idea of what had actually happened. The Editors' Law of October 4, 1933 (the law that cost Bella Fromm her job) had given Göbbels unprecedented power to muzzle editors and journalists. Consequently, newspapers carried abbreviated and sanitized accounts of the murders, explaining that Röhm and a handful of his henchmen had been shot for conduct besmirching Germany's good name. The newspaper *Deutsche Allgemeine Zeitung* assured its readers: "We now have a strong, consolidated and purified state. We need not dwell on the repulsive details which constituted the background of that pseudo revolution." The newspaper accounts may have puzzled some of the residents near Lichterfelde Barracks who clearly heard gunshots at twenty-minute intervals all day Saturday and Sunday. At Dietrich and Lippert's Münich trial, witnesses postulated a death toll that exceeded one thousand.

The Nazis were usually quite meticulous in their record-keeping. This was one notable exception.

A final observation. Hitler and the Nazi Party would never have achieved success without the essential ingredient of money—and when it came to fund-raising, Hitler had few peers. At one time Thomas Mann had dismissed him with the prediction, "He won't last eight months," but the renowned novelist was but one of many Germans who badly misjudged the future chancellor. While campaigning and wooing voters, Hitler portrayed himself as a friend of the working class; the stark difference between his words and his actions was demonstrated soon after he took office.

The Nazis proclaimed May 1, 1933 (May Day) a national holiday, and in a speech to 100,000 at Tempelhof Airfield, he stressed to the working-class crowd the importance of respect for workers. The very next day offices of trade unions throughout Germany were occupied, their leaders arrested. The unions were dissolved and their funds confiscated. Collective bargaining vanished into thin air, as did the right to strike. As a result of Hitler's betrayal, almost overnight the German worker had become a virtual serf.

Dr. Fritz Thyssen

Hitler replaced the unions with the Deutsche Arbeits-front (German Labour Front). The DAF was headed by Hitler crony Robert Ley, and developed into a mammoth bureaucracy with a hefty budget. This organization con-trolled—with strict regimentation—hiring and dismissal of workers, their insurance and compensation, as well as all matters related to working conditions. Ley ran the DAF with an iron hand with Hitler's blessing despite the fact that he was regarded as a coarse, eccentric anti-Semite and an alcoholic. (He ended up killing himself in his Nuremberg cell on October 24, 1945 as he awaited trial.)

During the period Hitler had been soliciting support from the working class, he was secretly meeting with a wealthy benefactor who hated unions—the Ruhr coal baron, Emil Kirdorf, who became a major source of finan-cial support for the fledgling Nazi Party. Kirdorf's contri-butions provided seed money for the development of the SA. But Kirdorf wasn't the only industrialist who suc-cumbed to Hitler's entreaties and was taken in by assur-ances that he would suppress Communism and neutralize unions while rebuilding the Wehrmacht (which would re-sult in generous profits).

Over the years Fritz Thyssen probably paid more money to Hitler personally than any other of the many coal and steel magnates who supported the Nazis. Thyssen was the founder of United Steel Works, the largest steel trust in the country, and was always ready to contribute to the needs of Hitler and his cause. How many millions of marks he handed over to Hitler will never be known. When Hitler needed funds to purchase the Barlow Palace (which became the Brown House), it was Emil Kirdorf who directed Rudolf Hess to Thyssen who quickly arranged a loan from a Rotterdam bank. As it turned out, Thyssen ended up paying off most of the loan. Later—

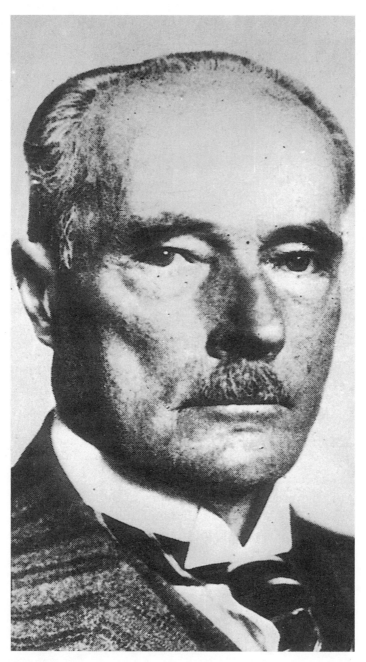
Gustav Krupp

when it was too late—Thyssen realized his tragic mistakes and fled to Switzerland at the onset of war in 1939.[1] He eventually found himself in a concentration camp after being arrested by Vichy authorities and returned to Germany from France.

As Germany's largest producer of armaments, Gustav Krupp had more than a passing interest in Hitler's pledge to restore the Fatherland's armed forces, and he didn't let the opportunity slip away. Initially wary, Krupp and Krupp's son Alfried were among Hitler's staunchest adherents and patrons. Gustav Krupp even added his signature to a petition which urged President von Hindenburg to relinquish the presidency to Hitler, but von Hindenburg ignored the petition. It was Gustav Krupp who suggested that the Reich Association of German Industry and the Union of German Employer Associations establish what was known as the Adolf Hitler Endowment of German Industry. The capitalists then channeled enormous sums of tax deductible money into this treasure trove on a quarterly basis. It is estimated that millions of marks were annually deposited into this private fund for the benefit of Hitler, who cleverly put Martin Bormann in charge of managing the funds. With the sycophantic Bormann holding the purse strings, Hitler assumed complete control of disbursements.

There was no shortage of donors among the German industrialists who seized the opportunities to protect—and enhance—their profitability by playing ball with Hitler while taking advantage of forced labor.

---

[1] From his sanctuary in Switzerland he sent a letter to Hitler in December 1939 claiming that his doubts about the Nazi regime began as a result of the treatment of Franz von Papen, and that his disaffection intensified with "the persecution of Christianity . . . the brutalization of its priests . . . the desecration of its churches." With Hitler, anyone who disagreed with him was his enemy.

Dr. Robert Ley

Friedrich Flick was one of the worst offenders when it came to exploiting slave laborers. Flick was on the board of many coal, iron, and steel works and paid large sums of money into Hitler's coffers. It has been estimated that 48,000 slave laborers toiled in Flick's various plants, of which 80 percent perished due to malnutrition and harsh treatment. Yet Flick always maintained that he had "neither a legal or moral obligation to make payment" for the use of forced labor. The influential Albert Vögler, general director of United Steel Works (Germany's biggest steel works) was a prime source of lucre for the Nazis. Other big money contributors from the realm of industry included Hugo Stinnes, Ernst Borsig, August Diehn, George von Schnitzler, August Rosterg, and Otto Wolf. The list was long. Significantly, in compiling the hit list for The Night of the Long Knives, their beneficiary—Adolf Hitler—was careful not to turn off any of the spigots of largesse. These industrialists helped pave the way for the man whose unconscionable actions led the world into a war that would claim fifty million lives.

EPILOGUE

The face of the world continues to shift uneasily. A United Nations "State of World Population" report advised: "On a scale unknown in history, people around the world are uprooting themselves and migrating in search of a better life." According to the report, international migration is setting the stage for explosive social tensions as various governments struggle to cope with the burgeoning problem. In the interval since that candid report was prepared, nothing has happened to alter that unsettling projection. If anything, the shift has attained accelerative proportions.

For affirmation of this trend we need only look at unified Germany, where an estimated five million migrants have relocated in the past decade. It is calculated that more than twenty-five thousand Afghans alone have moved into that country in the five years following the Taliban's seizure of power. The Muslim population in Germany now exceeds three and a half million. In some instances, cultural differences have engendered a resentment against non-Germans that has intensified since the merger of West Germany and East Germany, and political leaders are divided on how best to manage the problem.

"Germany for Germans" has become the battle cry of certain activists, a sentiment fueled by neo-Nazi elements.

In addressing the International Military Tribunal at Nuremberg, French prosecutor François de Menthon asked:

> How can one explain how Germany, fertilized through the centuries by classic antiquity and Christianity, by the ideals of liberty, equality, and social justice, by the common heritage of western humanism to which she has brought such noble and precious contributions, could have come to this astonishing return to primitive barbarism?

In these pages I've made an effort to provide some answers to that troubling question, although a rational explanation remains elusive.

In the introduction, I asked: Could Hitler happen again? The unification has recast the political spectrum in Germany. The hostility directed toward "guest workers" and other immigrants has nurtured an atmosphere that creates opportunities for demagogic leadership that could exploit xenophobia, as well as latent prejudices and animosities. Although unlikely, a Hitler-type politician could conceivably emerge, slipping through an opening created by social and economic distress in an open political environment.

Hitler was an extremely adroit political maneuverer who knew how to capitalize on the angst associated with human frailty. He was the quintessential wheeler-dealer. It wasn't until he had duped the electorate and reached the top that he abandoned restraint and a feigned civility. And then it was too late. With Operation KOLIBRI he signaled his manifesto: His way, or death. The civilized world failed to grasp the enormity of his action and intent, and did not recognize that this was the blueprint for his subsequent modus operandi.

Could it happen again? To categorically dismiss that notion would indeed be imprudent. The collapse of the Union of Soviet Socialist Republics was not expected. But it happened, with astonishing swiftness. The disintegration of Yugoslavia was not expected. But it happened—and "ethnic cleansing" resulted.

In the denouement to his well-documented book, *Justice at Nuremberg,* Robert E. Conot wrote:

> Never let it be forgotten that Hitler exploited the freedom granted him by the Weimar Constitution to destroy the republic. The rise of a new Hitler in an industrial nation may be remote, but it is not impossible. Given the proper combination of circumstances, no country, including the United States, is immune.

Is there another Adolf Hitler lurking somewhere beneath the political surface? The path of history is strewn with remnants of the unthinkable. Perpetual vigilance is essential—and constant awareness of the past.

Bibliography

BOOKS:

Baur, Hans. *Hitler At My Side*. Houston: Eichler Publishing Co., 1986.

Beever, Antony. *The Fall of Berlin: 1945*. New York: Viking, 2002.

Bezymenski, Lev. *The Death of Adolf Hitler: Unknown Documents from Soviet Archives*. New York: Harcourt, Brace and World, 1968.

Bracher, Karl Dietrich. *The German Dictatorship*. New York: Praeger Publishers, Inc., 1970.

Bullock, Alan. *Hitler: A Study in Tyranny*. New York: Bantam, 1961.

Butler, Rupert. *The Black Angels: The Story of the Waffen-SS*. Middlesex, England: Hamlyn Publishing Group, Inc., 1978.

Calic, Edouard. *Reinhard Heydrich*. New York: William Morrow & Co., 1982.

Conot, Robert E. *Justice at Nuremberg*. New York: Carroll & Graf, 2000.

Cooper, Matthew. *The German Army: 1933–1945*. New York: Stein & Day, 1978.

Craig, Gordon A. *Germany 1866–1945*. Oxford: Oxford University Press, 1980.

Delarue, Jacques. *The Gestapo: A History of Horror.* New York: William Morrow & Co., 1964.

Dodd, Martha. *My Years in Germany.* London: Gollancz, 1939.

Dodd, William E. *Ambassador Dodd's Diary.* London: Gollancz, 1941.

Dornberg, John. *Münich 1923: The Story of Hitler's First Grab for Power.* New York: Harper & Row, 1982.

Farago, Ladislas. *Aftermath: Martin Bormann and the Fourth Reich.* New York: Simon & Schuster, 1974.

Fest, Joachim C. *The Face of the Third Reich.* New York: Pantheon Books, 1970.

———. *Hitler.* New York: Harcourt, Brace, Jovanovich, 1974.

Fischer, Klaus P. *Nazi Germany: A New History.* New York: The Continuum Publishing Co., 1995.

Frischauer, Willi. *The Rise and Fall of Hermann Göring.* Boston: Houghton Mifflin Co., 1951.

Fromm, Bella. *Blood and Banquets: A Berlin Social Diary.* New York: Garden City Publishing Co., 1944.

Galante, Pierre and Eugene Silianoff. *Voices from the Bunker.* New York: G. P. Putnam's Sons, 1989.

Gallo, Max. *The Night of Long Knives.* New York: Harper & Row, 1972.

Gisevius, Hans Bernd. *To the Bitter End.* Boston: Houghton Mifflin Co., 1947.

Görlitz, Walter. *History of the German General Staff, 1657–1945.* New York: Praeger Co., 1953.

Graber, G. S. *The Life and Times of Reinhard Heydrich.* New York: David McKay Co., Inc., 1980.

Grunberger, Richard. *Hitler's SS.* New York: Delacorte Press, 1971.

Hanfstängl, Ernst. *Unheard Witness.* New York: Lippincott Co., 1971.

Hanser, Richard. *Putsch: How Hitler Made a Revolution.* New York: Peter H. Wyden, 1970.

Hayman, Ronald. *Hitler & Geli.* New York & London: Bloomsbury Publishing, 1997.

Hecht, Ben. *A Child of the Century.* New York: Simon & Schuster, Inc., 1955.

Heiden, Konrad. *Der Führer.* Boston: Houghton Mifflin Co., 1944.

Infield, Glenn. *Eva and Adolf.* New York: Grosset & Dunlap, 1974.

Irving, David. *Goring.* New York: William Morrow & Co., Inc., 1989.

———. Hess: *The Missing Years.* London: Grafton Books, 1989.

Ivanov, Miroslav. *Target: Heydrich.* New York: The Macmillan Co., 1974.

Koch, H. W. *In the Name of the Volk: Political Justice in Hitler's Germany.* New York: Barnes & Noble Books, 1989.

Langer, Walter C. *The Mind of Adolf Hitler.* New York: Basic Books, Inc., 1972.

MacDonald, Callum. *The Killing of SS Obergruppenführer Reinhard Heydrich.* New York: Collier Books, 1990.

Machtan, Lothar. *The Hidden Hitler.* New York: Basic Books, 2001.

Macksey, Kenneth. *From Triumph to Disaster: The Fatal Flaws of German Generalship from Moltke to Guderian.* London: Greenhill Books, 1996.

Manchester, William. *The Arms of Krupp.* New York: Bantam Books, 1970.

Manvell, Roger and Heinrich Fränkel. *Dr. Göbbels: His Life and Death.* New York: Simon & Schuster, 1960.

————. *Hess.* London: MacGibbon and Kee, 1971.

————. *Himmler.* New York: Putnam, 1965.

————. *The Hundred Days to Hitler.* New York: St. Martin's Press, 1974.

Meissner, Hans-Otto. *Magda Göbbels: The First Lady of the Third Reich.* New York: The Dial Press, 1980.

Messenger, Charles. *Sepp Dietrich: Hitler's Gladiator.* London: Brassey's Defense Publishers, 1988.

Metcalfe, Philip. *1933.* New York: Harper & Row, 1989.

Middleman, Keith and John Barnes. *Baldwin: A Biography.* New York: The Macmillan Co., 1969.

Mondadori, Arnoldo. *Hitler: Pro & Con.* New York: Columbia House, 1971.

Mosley, Leonard. *The Reich Marshal: A Biography of Hermann Göring.* New York: Doubleday & Co., 1974.

Noakes, Jeremy and Geoffrey Pridham. *Nazism: A History in Documents and Eyewitness Accounts, 1919–1945.* New York: Schocken Books, 1990.

O'Donnell, James P. *The Bunker.* Boston: Houghton Mifflin Co., 1978.

Overy, Richard. *Interrogations: The Nazi Elite in Allied Hands, 1945.* New York: Viking, 2001.

Payne, Robert. *The Life and Death of Adolf Hitler.* New York: Praeger Co., 1973.

Petrova, Ada and Peter Watson. *The Death of Hitler.* New York: W. W. Norton & Co., Inc., 1995.

Prittie, Terence. *Adenauer: A Study in Fortitude.* Chicago: Cowles Book Co., Inc., 1971.

Richardi, Hans-Günter and Klaus Schumann. *Geheimakte Gerlich/Bell.* Münich: Ludwig Publications, 1993.

Schmidt, Matthias. *Albert Speer: The End of a Myth.* New York: St. Martin's Press, 1984.

Schwarzwaller, Wulf. *Rudolf Hess: The Last Nazi.* Bethesda: National Press, Inc., 1988.

————. *The Unknown Hitler: Behind the Image of History's Darkest Name.* New York: Berkley Books, 1990.

Sereny, Gitta. *Albert Speer: His Battle With Truth.* New York: Alfred A. Knopf, Inc., 1995.

Shirer, William L. *Berlin Diary: The Journal of a Foreign Correspondent 1934–1941.* New York: Alfred Knopf, 1941.

————. *The Rise and Fall of the Third Reich: A History of Nazi Germany.* New York: Simon & Schuster, 1960.

Speer, Albert. *Infiltration.* New York: The Macmillan Co., 1991.

————. *Inside the Third Reich.* New York: The Macmillan Co., 1970.

Stevenson, William. *The Bormann Brotherhood.* New York: Bantam Books, Inc., 1973.

Strasser, Otto and Michael Stern. *Flight from Terror.* New York: Robert M. McBride & Co., 1943.

Sweeting, C. G. *Hitler's Personal Pilot: The Life and Times of Hans Baur.* Washington, D.C./Dulles, Virginia: Brassey's Inc., 2000.

Thomas, W. Hugh. *The Murder of Rudolf Hess.* New York: Harper & Row, 1979.

Tobias, Fritz. *The Reichstag Fire.* New York: G. P. Putnam's Sons, 1964.

Toland, John. *Adolf Hitler.* New York: Doubleday & Co., Inc., 1976.

————. *The Last 100 Days.* New York: Random House, 1965.

Trevor-Roper, Hugh R. *The Last Days of Hitler.* New York: Macmillan Co., 1947.

Tusa, Ann and John Tusa. *The Nuremberg Trial.* New York: Atheneum, 1984.

Van Capelle, Henk and Peter van de Bovenkamp. *Hitler's Henchmen.* New York: Gallery Books, 1990.

Von Lang, Jochen. *The Secretary: Martin Bormann.* New York: Random House, 1979.

Weitz, John. *Hitler's Diplomat: The Life and Times of Joachim von Ribbentrop.* New York: Ticknor & Fields, 1992.

Whiting, Charles. *Massacre at Malmedy: The Story of Jochen Peiper's Battle Group Ardennes, December 1944.* New York: Stein & Day, 1971.

Wighton, Charles. *Heydrich: Hitler's Most Evil Henchman.* Philadelphia: Chilton Book Company, 1962.

Wistrich, Robert. *Who's Who in Nazi Germany.* New York: Bonanza Books, 1984.

Young, Desmond. *Rommel: The Desert Fox.* New York: Harper Brothers, 1950.

PUBLICATIONS:

Friedrich, Otto. "When Darkness Fell." *Time,* August 28, 1989 (Fiftieth Anniversary Special Issue).

Keegan, John. "Fifty Years Later." *U.S. News & World Report,* September 4, 1989 (World War II Special Issue).

Kramer, Jane. "Private Lives: Germany's Troubled War on Terrorism (Letter from Europe)." *The New Yorker,* February 11, 2002.

Rich, Frank. "Reliving the Nazi Nightmare." *Time,* April 17, 1978.

Index

217